Year 11 ATAR Music

Student Workbook

SARAH STOPHER

ISBN-13: 978-1508723813
ISBN-10: 1508723818

Printed in the United States of America
First Printing: January 2015

Cover image © Jelen80 | Dreamstime.com

www.stophermusic.com

Contents

Section 1: Aural

Lesson 1

Interval Recognition (13 marks)
a) Listen to the recording and add the missing notes. Identify the intervals as marked.

1. _____ 2. _____ 3. _____ 4. _____

b) Listen to the excerpt and name the harmonic interval on the last note. _____

Discrepancies (8 marks)
Listen to the recording and identify the discrepancies. Write the corrections only in the stave above.
Prior to the recording commencing the beat will be played on a woodblock.

Rhythmic Dictation (16 marks)
Listen to the recording and notate the rhythm for the pitches provided. Prior to the recording
commencing the beat will be played on a woodblock.

Modulation (1 mark)
Listening to the recording and identify any modulations.

No modulation _____   Relative major _____

Relative minor _____   Dominant _____

Scale Recognition (3 marks)

Listening to the recording and identify the two scales as major, harmonic minor, major pentatonic, minor pentatonic, chromatic or blues.

1. _____   2. _____

3. _____

Pitch Dictation (20 marks)

Listen to the recording and notate the pitch for the rhythm provided. Prior to the recording commencing the beat will be played on a woodblock and the tonic triad on the piano.

Melodic Dictation (21 marks)

Listen to the recording and notate the melody. Prior to the recording commencing the beat will be played on a woodblock and the tonic triad on the piano.

Chord Recognition (4 marks)

Listening to the recording and identify the four chords as major, minor, augmented or diminished.

1. _____   2. _____   3. _____   4. _____

Harmonic Progression (12 marks)

Listen to the recording and idenfity the chords used in this progression. The tonic will be played prior to the excerpt starting. Name the cadence at the end of each excerpt.

Cadence: _____   Cadence: _____

TOTAL MARKS   **/98**   **CONVERTED**   **%**

Lesson 2

Interval Recognition (13 marks)

a) Listen to the recording and add the missing notes. Identify the intervals as marked.

1._____ 2._____ 3._____ 4._____

b) Listen to the excerpt and name the harmonic interval on the last note. _____

Discrepancies (8 marks)

Listen to the recording and identify the discrepancies. Write the corrections only in the stave above.
Prior to the recording commencing the beat will be played on a woodblock.

Rhythmic Dictation (16 marks)

Listen to the recording and notate the rhythm for the pitches provided. Prior to the recording
commencing the beat will be played on a woodblock.

Modulation (1 mark)

Listening to the recording and identify any modulations.

No modulation _____   Relative major _____

Relative minor _____   Dominant _____

Scale Recognition (3 marks)

Listening to the recording and identify the two scales as major, harmonic minor, major pentatonic, minor pentatonic, chromatic or blues.

1._____   2._____

3._____

Pitch Dictation (15 marks)

Listen to the recording and notate the pitch for the rhythm provided. Prior to the recording commencing the beat will be played on a woodblock and the tonic triad on the piano.

Melodic Dictation (20 marks)

Listen to the recording and notate the melody. Prior to the recording commencing the beat will be played on a woodblock and the tonic triad on the piano.

Chord Recognition (4 marks)

Listening to the recording and identify the four chords as major, minor, augmented or diminished.

1._____   2._____   3._____   4._____

Harmonic Progression (12 marks)

Listen to the recording and idenfity the chords used in this progression. The tonic will be played prior to the excerpt starting. Name the cadence at the end of each excerpt.

Cadence: _____   Cadence: _____

TOTAL MARKS   /92   CONVERTED   %

Lesson 3

Interval Recognition (13 marks)
a) Listen to the recording and add the missing notes. Identify the intervals as marked.

1. _____   2. _____   3. _____   4. _____

b) Listen to the excerpt and name the harmonic interval on the last note. _____

Discrepancies (8 marks)
Listen to the recording and identify the discrepancies. Write the corrections only in the stave above.
Prior to the recording commencing the beat will be played on a woodblock.

Rhythmic Dictation (11 marks)
Listen to the recording and notate the rhythm for the pitches provided. Prior to the recording
commencing the beat will be played on a woodblock.

Modulation (1 mark)
Listening to the recording and identify any modulations.

No modulation _____   Relative major _____

Relative minor _____   Dominant _____

Scale Recognition (3 marks)

Listening to the recording and identify the three scales as major, harmonic minor, major pentatonic, minor pentatonic, chromatic or blues.

1. _____ 2. _____

3. _____

Pitch Dictation (25 marks)

Listen to the recording and notate the pitch for the rhythm provided. Prior to the recording commencing the beat will be played on a woodblock and the tonic triad on the piano.

Melodic Dictation (16 marks)

Listen to the recording and notate the melody. Prior to the recording commencing the beat will be played on a woodblock and the tonic triad on the piano.

Chord Recognition (4 marks)

Listening to the recording and identify the four chords as major, minor, augmented or diminished.

1. _____   2. _____   3. _____   4. _____

Harmonic Progression (12 marks)

Listen to the recording and idenfity the chords used in this progression. The tonic will be played prior to the excerpt starting. Name the cadence at the end of each excerpt.

Cadence: _____   Cadence: _____

TOTAL MARKS   **/93**   **CONVERTED**   **%**

Lesson 4

Interval Recognition (13 marks)

a) Listen to the recording and add the missing notes. Identify the intervals as marked.

1._____   2._____   3._____   4._____

b) Listen to the excerpt and name the harmonic interval on the last note. _____

Discrepancies (8 marks)

Listen to the recording and identify the discrepancies. Write the corrections only in the stave above.
Prior to the recording commencing the beat will be played on a woodblock.

Rhythmic Dictation (8 marks)

Listen to the recording and notate the rhythm for the pitches provided. Prior to the recording
commencing the beat will be played on a woodblock.

Modulation (1 mark)

Listening to the recording and identify any modulations.

No modulation _____   Relative major _____

Relative minor _____   Dominant _____

Scale Recognition (3 marks)

Listening to the recording and identify the two scales as major, harmonic minor, major pentatonic, minor pentatonic, chromatic or blues.

1. _____   2. _____

3. _____

Pitch Dictation (20 marks)

Listen to the recording and notate the pitch for the rhythm provided. Prior to the recording commencing the beat will be played on a woodblock and the tonic triad on the piano.

Melodic Dictation (20 marks)

Listen to the recording and notate the melody. Prior to the recording commencing the beat will be played on a woodblock and the tonic triad on the piano.

Chord Recognition (4 marks)

Listening to the recording and identify the four chords as major, minor, augmented or diminished.

1. _____   2. _____   3. _____   4. _____

Harmonic Progression (12 marks)

Listen to the recording and idenfity the chords used in this progression. The tonic will be played prior to the excerpt starting. Name the cadence at the end of each excerpt.

Cadence: _____   Cadence: _____

TOTAL MARKS   **/89**   **CONVERTED**   **%**

Lesson 5

Interval Recognition (13 marks)
a) Listen to the recording and add the missing notes. Identify the intervals as marked.

1. _____ 2. _____ 3. _____ 4. _____

b) Listen to the excerpt and name the harmonic interval on the last note. _____

Discrepancies (8 marks)
Listen to the recording and identify the discrepancies. Write the corrections only in the stave above.
Prior to the recording commencing the beat will be played on a woodblock.

Rhythmic Dictation (8 marks)
Listen to the recording and notate the rhythm for the pitches provided. Prior to the recording
commencing the beat will be played on a woodblock.

Modulation (1 mark)
Listening to the recording and identify any modulations.

No modulation _____   Relative major _____

Relative minor _____   Dominant   ___ ___

Scale Recognition (3 marks)

Listening to the recording and identify the two scales as major, harmonic minor, major pentatonic, minor pentatonic, chromatic or blues.

1. _____   2. _____

3. _____

Pitch Dictation (17 marks)

Listen to the recording and notate the pitch for the rhythm provided. Prior to the recording commencing the beat will be played on a woodblock and the tonic triad on the piano.

Melodic Dictation (21 marks)

Listen to the recording and notate the melody. Prior to the recording commencing the beat will be played on a woodblock and the tonic triad on the piano.

Chord Recognition (4 marks)

Listening to the recording and identify the four chords as major, minor, augmented or diminished.

1. _____   2. _____   3. _____   4. _____

Harmonic Progression (12 marks)

Listen to the recording and idenfity the chords used in this progression. The tonic will be played prior to the excerpt starting. Name the cadence at the end of each excerpt.

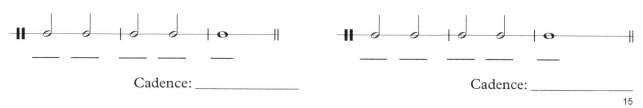

Cadence: _____   Cadence: _____

TOTAL MARKS   **/87**   **CONVERTED**   **%**

Lesson 6

Interval Recognition (13 marks)

a) Listen to the recording and add the missing notes. Identify the intervals as marked.

1. _____ 2. _____ 3. _____ 4. _____

b) Listen to the excerpt and name the harmonic interval on the last note. _____

Discrepancies (8 marks)

Listen to the recording and identify the discrepancies. Write the corrections only in the stave above. Prior to the recording commencing the beat will be played on a woodblock.

Rhythmic Dictation (16 marks)

Listen to the recording and notate the rhythm for the pitches provided. Prior to the recording commencing the beat will be played on a woodblock.

Modulation (1 mark)

Listening to the recording and identify any modulations.

No modulation _____   Relative major _____

Relative minor _____   Dominant _____

Scale Recognition (3 marks)

Listening to the recording and identify the two scales as major, harmonic minor, major pentatonic, minor pentatonic, chromatic or blues.

1. _____   2. _____

3. _____

Pitch Dictation (17 marks)

Listen to the recording and notate the pitch for the rhythm provided. Prior to the recording commencing the beat will be played on a woodblock and the tonic triad on the piano.

Melodic Dictation (17 marks)

Listen to the recording and notate the melody. Prior to the recording commencing the beat will be played on a woodblock and the tonic triad on the piano.

Chord Recognition (4 marks)

Listening to the recording and identify the four chords as major, minor, augmented or diminished.

1. _____   2. _____   3. _____   4. _____

Harmonic Progression (12 marks)

Listen to the recording and idenfity the chords used in this progression. The tonic will be played prior to the excerpt starting. Name the cadence at the end of each excerpt.

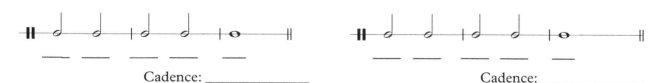

Cadence: _____   Cadence: _____

TOTAL MARKS   **/91**   **CONVERTED**   **%**

Lesson 7

Interval Recognition (13 marks)

a) Listen to the recording and add the missing notes. Identify the intervals as marked.

1._____   2._____   3._____   4._____

b) Listen to the excerpt and name the harmonic interval on the last note. _____

Discrepancies (8 marks)

Listen to the recording and identify the discrepancies. Write the corrections only in the stave above.
Prior to the recording commencing the beat will be played on a woodblock.

Rhythmic Dictation (16 marks)

Listen to the recording and notate the rhythm for the pitches provided. Prior to the recording
commencing the beat will be played on a woodblock.

Modulation (1 mark)

Listening to the recording and identify any modulations.

No modulation   _____   Relative major   _____

Relative minor   _____   Dominant   _____

Scale Recognition (3 marks)

Listening to the recording and identify the two scales as major, harmonic minor, major pentatonic, minor pentatonic, chromatic or blues.

1. _____   2. _____

3. _____

Pitch Dictation (12 marks)

Listen to the recording and notate the pitch for the rhythm provided. Prior to the recording commencing the beat will be played on a woodblock and the tonic triad on the piano.

Melodic Dictation (19 marks)

Listen to the recording and notate the melody. Prior to the recording commencing the beat will be played on a woodblock and the tonic triad on the piano.

Chord Recognition (4 marks)

Listening to the recording and identify the four chords as major, minor, augmented or diminished.

1. _____   2. _____   3. _____   4. _____

Harmonic Progression (12 marks)

Listen to the recording and idenfity the chords used in this progression. The tonic will be played prior to the excerpt starting. Name the cadence at the end of each excerpt.

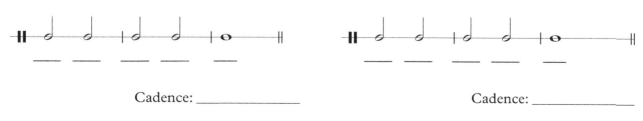

Cadence: _____   Cadence: _____

TOTAL MARKS   /88   **CONVERTED**   %

Lesson 8

Interval Recognition (13 marks)

a) Listen to the recording and add the missing notes. Identify the intervals as marked.

1. _____ 2. _____ 3. _____ 4. _____

b) Listen to the excerpt and name the harmonic interval on the last note. _____

Discrepancies (8 marks)

Listen to the recording and identify the discrepancies. Write the corrections only in the stave above.
Prior to the recording commencing the beat will be played on a woodblock.

Rhythmic Dictation (16 marks)

Listen to the recording and notate the rhythm for the pitches provided. Prior to the recording
commencing the beat will be played on a woodblock.

Modulation (1 mark)

Listening to the recording and identify any modulations.

No modulation _____   Relative major _____

Relative minor _____   Dominant _____

Scale Recognition (3 marks)

Listening to the recording and identify the two scales as major, harmonic minor, major pentatonic, minor pentatonic, chromatic or blues.

1. _____   2. _____

3. _____

Pitch Dictation (20 marks)

Listen to the recording and notate the pitch for the rhythm provided. Prior to the recording commencing the beat will be played on a woodblock and the tonic triad on the piano.

Melodic Dictation (18 marks)

Listen to the recording and notate the melody. Prior to the recording commencing the beat will be played on a woodblock and the tonic triad on the piano.

Chord Recognition (4 marks)

Listening to the recording and identify the four chords as major, minor, augmented or diminished.

1. _____   2. _____   3. _____   4. _____

Harmonic Progression (12 marks)

Listen to the recording and idenfity the chords used in this progression. The tonic will be played prior to the excerpt starting. Name the cadence at the end of each excerpt.

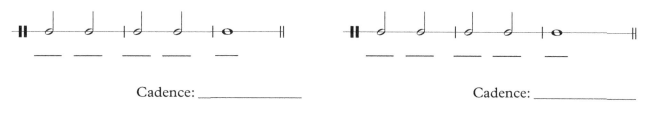

Cadence: _____   Cadence: _____

TOTAL MARKS   /95   **CONVERTED**   %

Lesson 9

Interval Recognition (13 marks)

a) Listen to the recording and add the missing notes. Identify the intervals as marked.

1. _____ 2. _____ 3. _____ 4. _____

b) Listen to the excerpt and name the harmonic interval on the last note. _____

Discrepancies (8 marks)

Listen to the recording and identify the discrepancies. Write the corrections only in the stave above.
Prior to the recording commencing the beat will be played on a woodblock.

Rhythmic Dictation (12 marks)

Listen to the recording and notate the rhythm for the pitches provided. Prior to the recording
commencing the beat will be played on a woodblock.

Modulation (1 mark)

Listening to the recording and identify any modulations.

No modulation _____   Relative major _____

Relative minor _____   Dominant _____

Scale Recognition (3 marks)

Listening to the recording and identify the two scales as major, harmonic minor, major pentatonic, minor pentatonic, chromatic or blues.

1._____ 2._____

3._____

Pitch Dictation (17 marks)

Listen to the recording and notate the pitch for the rhythm provided. Prior to the recording commencing the beat will be played on a woodblock and the tonic triad on the piano.

Melodic Dictation (13 marks)

Listen to the recording and notate the melody. Prior to the recording commencing the beat will be played on a woodblock and the tonic triad on the piano.

Chord Recognition (4 marks)

Listening to the recording and identify the four chords as major, minor, augmented or diminished.

1._____ 2._____ 3._____ 4._____

Harmonic Progression (12 marks)

Listen to the recording and idenfity the chords used in this progression. The tonic will be played prior to the excerpt starting. Name the cadence at the end of each excerpt.

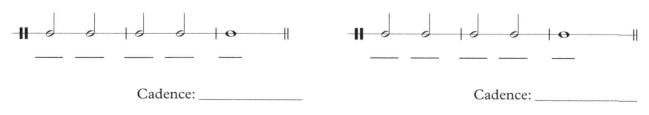

Cadence: _____ Cadence: _____

TOTAL MARKS **/83** **CONVERTED** **%**

Lesson 10

Interval Recognition (13 marks)
a) Listen to the recording and add the missing notes. Identify the intervals as marked.

1. _____   2. _____   3. _____   4. _____

b) Listen to the excerpt and name the harmonic interval on the last note. _____

Discrepancies (8 marks)
Listen to the recording and identify the discrepancies. Write the corrections only in the stave above.
Prior to the recording commencing the beat will be played on a woodblock.

Rhythmic Dictation (8 marks)
Listen to the recording and notate the rhythm for the pitches provided. Prior to the recording
commencing the beat will be played on a woodblock.

Modulation (1 mark)
Listening to the recording and identify any modulations.

No modulation _____   Relative major _____

Relative minor _____   Dominant _____

Scale Recognition (3 marks)

Listening to the recording and identify the two scales as major, harmonic minor, major pentatonic, minor pentatonic, chromatic or blues.

1. _____ 2. _____

3. _____

Pitch Dictation (16 marks)

Listen to the recording and notate the pitch for the rhythm provided. Prior to the recording commencing the beat will be played on a woodblock and the tonic triad on the piano.

Melodic Dictation (14 marks)

Listen to the recording and notate the melody. Prior to the recording commencing the beat will be played on a woodblock and the tonic triad on the piano.

Chord Recognition (4 marks)

Listening to the recording and identify the four chords as major, minor, augmented or diminished.

1. _____   2. _____   3. _____   4. _____

Harmonic Progression (12 marks)

Listen to the recording and idenfity the chords used in this progression. The tonic will be played prior to the excerpt starting. Name the cadence at the end of each excerpt.

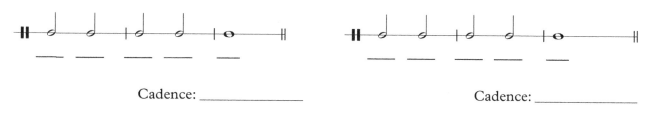

Cadence: _____   Cadence: _____

TOTAL MARKS   **/79**   **CONVERTED**   **%**

Lesson 11

Interval Recognition (13 marks)

a) Listen to the recording and add the missing notes. Identify the intervals as marked.

1. _____   2. _____   3. _____   4. _____

b) Listen to the excerpt and name the harmonic interval on the last note. _____

Discrepancies (8 marks)

Listen to the recording and identify the discrepancies. Write the corrections only in the stave above.
Prior to the recording commencing the beat will be played on a woodblock.

Rhythmic Dictation (16 marks)

Listen to the recording and notate the rhythm for the pitches provided. Prior to the recording
commencing the beat will be played on a woodblock.

Modulation (1 mark)

Listening to the recording and identify any modulations.

No modulation _____   Relative major _____

Relative minor _____   Dominant _____

Scale Recognition (3 marks)

Listening to the recording and identify the two scales as major, harmonic minor, major pentatonic, minor pentatonic, chromatic or blues.

1. _____   2. _____

3. _____

Pitch Dictation (18 marks)

Listen to the recording and notate the pitch for the rhythm provided. Prior to the recording commencing the beat will be played on a woodblock and the tonic triad on the piano.

Melodic Dictation (18 marks)

Listen to the recording and notate the melody. Prior to the recording commencing the beat will be played on a woodblock and the tonic triad on the piano.

Chord Recognition (4 marks)

Listening to the recording and identify the four chords as major, minor, augmented or diminished.

1. _____   2. _____   3. _____   4. _____

Harmonic Progression (12 marks)

Listen to the recording and idenfity the chords used in this progression. The tonic will be played prior to the excerpt starting. Name the cadence at the end of each excerpt.

Cadence: _____   Cadence: _____

TOTAL MARKS   **/93**   **CONVERTED**   **%**

Lesson 12

Interval Recognition (13 marks)

a) Listen to the recording and add the missing notes. Identify the intervals as marked.

1._____ 2._____ 3._____ 4._____

b) Listen to the excerpt and name the harmonic interval on the last note. _____

Discrepancies (8 marks)

Listen to the recording and identify the discrepancies. Write the corrections only in the stave above.
Prior to the recording commencing the beat will be played on a woodblock.

Rhythmic Dictation (8 marks)

Listen to the recording and notate the rhythm for the pitches provided. Prior to the recording
commencing the beat will be played on a woodblock.

Modulation (1 mark)

Listening to the recording and identify any modulations.

No modulation _____   Relative major _____

Relative minor _____   Dominant _____

Scale Recognition (3 marks)

Listening to the recording and identify the two scales as major, harmonic minor, major pentatonic, minor pentatonic, chromatic or blues.

1. _____   2. _____

3. _____

Pitch Dictation (17 marks)

Listen to the recording and notate the pitch for the rhythm provided. Prior to the recording commencing the beat will be played on a woodblock and the tonic triad on the piano.

Melodic Dictation (20 marks)

Listen to the recording and notate the melody. Prior to the recording commencing the beat will be played on a woodblock and the tonic triad on the piano.

Chord Recognition (4 marks)

Listening to the recording and identify the four chords as major, minor, augmented or diminished.

1. _____   2. _____   3. _____   4. _____

Harmonic Progression (12 marks)

Listen to the recording and idenfity the chords used in this progression. The tonic will be played prior to the excerpt starting. Name the cadence at the end of each excerpt.

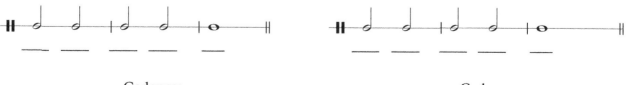

Cadence: _____   Cadence: _____

TOTAL MARKS   **/86**   **CONVERTED**   **%**

Lesson 13

Interval Recognition (13 marks)

a) Listen to the recording and add the missing notes. Identify the intervals as marked.

1._____ 2._____ 3._____ 4._____

b) Listen to the excerpt and name the harmonic interval on the last note. _____

Discrepancies (8 marks)

Listen to the recording and identify the discrepancies. Write the corrections only in the stave above. Prior to the recording commencing the beat will be played on a woodblock.

Rhythmic Dictation (8 marks)

Listen to the recording and notate the rhythm for the pitches provided. Prior to the recording commencing the beat will be played on a woodblock.

Modulation (1 mark)

Listening to the recording and identify any modulations.

No modulation _____   Relative major _____

Relative minor _____   Dominant _____

Scale Recognition (3 marks)

Listening to the recording and identify the two scales as major, harmonic minor, major pentatonic, minor pentatonic, chromatic or blues.

1. _____   2. _____

3. _____

Pitch Dictation (15 marks)

Listen to the recording and notate the pitch for the rhythm provided. Prior to the recording commencing the beat will be played on a woodblock and the tonic triad on the piano.

Melodic Dictation (13 marks)

Listen to the recording and notate the melody. Prior to the recording commencing the beat will be played on a woodblock and the tonic triad on the piano.

Chord Recognition (4 marks)

Listening to the recording and identify the four chords as major, minor, augmented or diminished.

1. _____   2. _____   3. _____   4. _____

Harmonic Progression (12 marks)

Listen to the recording and idenfity the chords used in this progression. The tonic will be played prior to the excerpt starting. Name the cadence at the end of each excerpt.

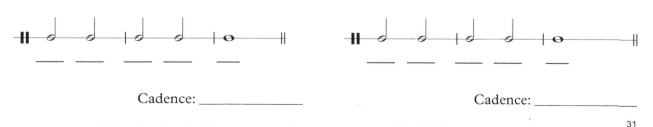

Cadence: _____   Cadence: _____

TOTAL MARKS   /77   **CONVERTED**   %

Lesson 14

Interval Recognition (13 marks)

a) Listen to the recording and add the missing notes. Identify the intervals as marked.

1. _____ 2. _____ 3. _____ 4. _____

b) Listen to the excerpt and name the harmonic interval on the last note. _____

Discrepancies (8 marks)

Listen to the recording and identify the discrepancies. Write the corrections only in the stave above. Prior to the recording commencing the beat will be played on a woodblock.

Rhythmic Dictation (8 marks)

Listen to the recording and notate the rhythm for the pitches provided. Prior to the recording commencing the beat will be played on a woodblock.

Modulation (1 mark)

Listening to the recording and identify any modulations.

No modulation _____   Relative major _____

Relative minor _____   Dominant _____

Scale Recognition (3 marks)

Listening to the recording and identify the two scales as major, harmonic minor, major pentatonic, minor pentatonic, chromatic or blues.

1. _____   2. _____

3. _____

Pitch Dictation (9 marks)

Listen to the recording and notate the pitch for the rhythm provided. Prior to the recording commencing the beat will be played on a woodblock and the tonic triad on the piano.

Melodic Dictation (17 marks)

Listen to the recording and notate the melody. Prior to the recording commencing the beat will be played on a woodblock and the tonic triad on the piano.

Chord Recognition (4 marks)

Listening to the recording and identify the four chords as major, minor, augmented or diminished.

1. _____   2. _____   3. _____   4. _____

Harmonic Progression (12 marks)

Listen to the recording and idenfity the chords used in this progression. The tonic will be played prior to the excerpt starting. Name the cadence at the end of each excerpt.

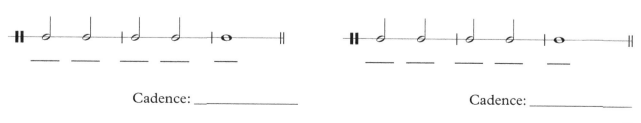

Cadence: _____   Cadence: _____

TOTAL MARKS   /75   CONVERTED   %

Lesson 15

Interval Recognition (13 marks)

a) Listen to the recording and add the missing notes. Identify the intervals as marked.

1. _____ 2. _____ 3. _____ 4. _____

b) Listen to the excerpt and name the harmonic interval on the last note. _____

Discrepancies (8 marks)

Listen to the recording and identify the discrepancies. Write the corrections only in the stave above.
Prior to the recording commencing the beat will be played on a woodblock.

Rhythmic Dictation (8 marks)

Listen to the recording and notate the rhythm for the pitches provided. Prior to the recording
commencing the beat will be played on a woodblock.

Modulation (1 mark)

Listening to the recording and identify any modulations.

No modulation _____   Relative major _____

Relative minor _____   Dominant _____

Scale Recognition (3 marks)

Listening to the recording and identify the two scales as major, harmonic minor, major pentatonic, minor pentatonic, chromatic or blues.

1. _____   2. _____

3. _____

Pitch Dictation (14 marks)

Listen to the recording and notate the pitch for the rhythm provided. Prior to the recording commencing the beat will be played on a woodblock and the tonic triad on the piano.

Melodic Dictation (18 marks)

Listen to the recording and notate the melody. Prior to the recording commencing the beat will be played on a woodblock and the tonic triad on the piano.

Chord Recognition (4 marks)

Listening to the recording and identify the four chords as major, minor, augmented or diminished.

1. _____   2. _____   3. _____   4. _____

Harmonic Progression (12 marks)

Listen to the recording and idenfity the chords used in this progression. The tonic will be played prior to the excerpt starting. Name the cadence at the end of each excerpt.

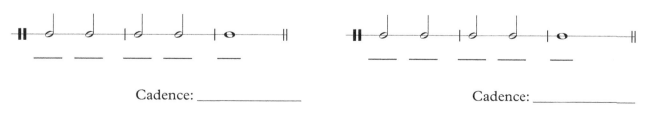

Cadence: _____   Cadence: _____

TOTAL MARKS   **/81**   **CONVERTED**   **%**

Lesson 16

Interval Recognition (13 marks)

a) Listen to the recording and add the missing notes. Identify the intervals as marked.

1. _____ 2. _____ 3. _____ 4. _____

b) Listen to the excerpt and name the harmonic interval on the last note. _____

Discrepancies (8 marks)

Listen to the recording and identify the discrepancies. Write the corrections only in the stave above.
Prior to the recording commencing the beat will be played on a woodblock.

Rhythmic Dictation (8 marks)

Listen to the recording and notate the rhythm for the pitches provided. Write in the barlines. Prior to the
recording commencing the beat will be played on a woodblock.

Modulation (1 mark)

Listening to the recording and identify any modulations.

No modulation   _____   Relative major   _____

Relative minor   _____   Dominant   _____

Scale Recognition (3 marks)

Listening to the recording and identify the two scales as major, harmonic minor, major pentatonic, minor pentatonic, chromatic or blues.

1. _____   2. _____

3. _____   _____

Pitch Dictation (13 marks)

Listen to the recording and notate the pitch for the rhythm provided. Prior to the recording commencing the beat will be played on a woodblock and the tonic triad on the piano.

Melodic Dictation (18 marks)

Listen to the recording and notate the melody. Prior to the recording commencing the beat will be played on a woodblock and the tonic triad on the piano.

Chord Recognition (4 marks)

Listening to the recording and identify the four chords as major, minor, augmented or diminished.

1. _____   2. _____   3. _____   4. _____

Harmonic Progression (12 marks)

Listen to the recording and idenfity the chords used in this progression. The tonic will be played prior to the excerpt starting. Name the cadence at the end of each excerpt.

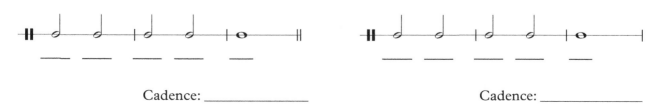

Cadence: _____   Cadence: _____

TOTAL MARKS   **/80**   **CONVERTED**   **%**

Lesson 17

Interval Recognition (13 marks)
a) Listen to the recording and add the missing notes. Identify the intervals as marked.

1._____ 2._____ 3._____ 4._____

b) Listen to the excerpt and name the harmonic interval on the last note. _____

Discrepancies (8 marks)
Listen to the recording and identify the discrepancies. Write the corrections only in the stave above.
Prior to the recording commencing the beat will be played on a woodblock.

Rhythmic Dictation (8 marks)
Listen to the recording and notate the rhythm for the pitches provided. Write in the barlines. Prior to the
recording commencing the beat will be played on a woodblock.

Modulation (1 mark)
Listening to the recording and identify any modulations.

No modulation   _____   Relative major   _____

Relative minor   _____   Dominant   _____

Scale Recognition (3 marks)

Listening to the recording and identify the two scales as major, harmonic minor, major pentatonic, minor pentatonic, chromatic or blues.

1. _____   2. _____

3. _____

Pitch Dictation (14 marks)

Listen to the recording and notate the pitch for the rhythm provided. Prior to the recording commencing the beat will be played on a woodblock and the tonic triad on the piano.

Melodic Dictation (12 marks)

Listen to the recording and notate the melody. Prior to the recording commencing the beat will be played on a woodblock and the tonic triad on the piano.

Chord Recognition (4 marks)

Listening to the recording and identify the four chords as major, minor, augmented or diminished.

1. _____   2. _____   3. _____   4. _____

Harmonic Progression (12 marks)

Listen to the recording and idenfity the chords used in this progression. The tonic will be played prior to the excerpt starting. Name the cadence at the end of each excerpt.

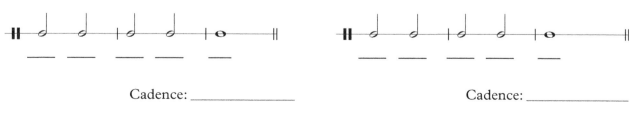

Cadence: _____   Cadence: _____

TOTAL MARKS   /75   **CONVERTED**   %

Lesson 18

Interval Recognition (13 marks)

a) Listen to the recording and add the missing notes. Identify the intervals as marked.

1. _____ 2. _____ 3. _____ 4. _____

b) Listen to the excerpt and name the harmonic interval on the last note. _____

Discrepancies (8 marks)

Listen to the recording and identify the discrepancies. Write the corrections only in the stave above. Prior to the recording commencing the beat will be played on a woodblock.

Rhythmic Dictation (10 marks)

Listen to the recording and notate the rhythm for the pitches provided. Write in the barlines. Prior to the recording commencing the beat will be played on a woodblock.

Modulation (1 mark)

Listening to the recording and identify any modulations.

No modulation _____   Relative major _____

Relative minor _____   Dominant _____

Scale Recognition (3 marks)

Listening to the recording and identify the two scales as major, harmonic minor, major pentatonic, minor pentatonic, chromatic or blues.

1. _____   2. _____

3. _____

Pitch Dictation (17 marks)

Listen to the recording and notate the pitch for the rhythm provided. Prior to the recording commencing the beat will be played on a woodblock and the tonic triad on the piano.

Melodic Dictation (17 marks)

Listen to the recording and notate the melody. Prior to the recording commencing the beat will be played on a woodblock and the tonic triad on the piano.

Chord Recognition (4 marks)

Listening to the recording and identify the four chords as major, minor, augmented or diminished.

1. _____   2. _____   3. _____   4. _____

Harmonic Progression (12 marks)

Listen to the recording and idenfity the chords used in this progression. The tonic will be played prior to the excerpt starting. Name the cadence at the end of each excerpt.

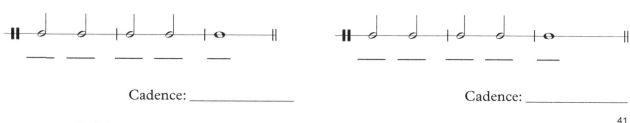

       Cadence: _____   Cadence: _____

TOTAL MARKS   **/85**   **CONVERTED**   **%**

Lesson 19

Interval Recognition (13 marks)

a) Listen to the recording and add the missing notes. Identify the intervals as marked.

1._____   2._____   3._____   4._____

b) Listen to the excerpt and name the harmonic interval on the last note. _____

Discrepancies (8 marks)

Listen to the recording and identify the discrepancies. Write the corrections only in the stave above.
Prior to the recording commencing the beat will be played on a woodblock.

Rhythmic Dictation (10 marks)

Listen to the recording and notate the rhythm for the pitches provided. Write in the barlines. Prior to the
recording commencing the beat will be played on a woodblock.

Modulation (1 mark)

Listening to the recording and identify any modulations.

No modulation   _____   Relative major   _____

Relative minor   _____   Dominant   _____

Scale Recognition (3 marks)

Listening to the recording and identify the two scales as major, harmonic minor, major pentatonic, minor pentatonic, chromatic or blues.

1. _____   2. _____

3. _____

Pitch Dictation (16 marks)

Listen to the recording and notate the pitch for the rhythm provided. Prior to the recording commencing the beat will be played on a woodblock and the tonic triad on the piano.

Melodic Dictation (18 marks)

Listen to the recording and notate the melody. Prior to the recording commencing the beat will be played on a woodblock and the tonic triad on the piano.

Chord Recognition (4 marks)

Listening to the recording and identify the four chords as major, minor, augmented or diminished.

1. _____   2. _____   3. _____   4. _____

Harmonic Progression (12 marks)

Listen to the recording and idenfity the chords used in this progression. The tonic will be played prior to the excerpt starting. Name the cadence at the end of each excerpt.

Cadence: _____   Cadence: _____

TOTAL MARKS   /85   CONVERTED   %

Lesson 20

Interval Recognition (13 marks)
a) Listen to the recording and add the missing notes. Identify the intervals as marked.

1. _____   2. _____   3. _____   4. _____

b) Listen to the excerpt and name the harmonic interval on the last note. _____

Discrepancies (8 marks)
Listen to the recording and identify the discrepancies. Write the corrections only in the stave above.
Prior to the recording commencing the beat will be played on a woodblock.

Rhythmic Dictation (10 marks)
Listen to the recording and notate the rhythm for the pitches provided. Write in the barlines. Prior to the
recording commencing the beat will be played on a woodblock.

Modulation (1 mark)
Listening to the recording and identify any modulations.

No modulation	_____	Relative major	_____
Relative minor	_____	Dominant	_____

Scale Recognition (3 marks)

Listening to the recording and identify the two scales as major, harmonic minor, major pentatonic, minor pentatonic, chromatic or blues.

1. _____   2. _____

3. _____

Pitch Dictation (17 marks)

Listen to the recording and notate the pitch for the rhythm provided. Prior to the recording commencing the beat will be played on a woodblock and the tonic triad on the piano.

Melodic Dictation (10 marks)

Listen to the recording and notate the melody. Prior to the recording commencing the beat will be played on a woodblock and the tonic triad on the piano.

Chord Recognition (4 marks)

Listening to the recording and identify the four chords as major, minor, augmented or diminished.

1. _____   2. _____   3. _____   4. _____

Harmonic Progression (12 marks)

Listen to the recording and idenfity the chords used in this progression. The tonic will be played prior to the excerpt starting. Name the cadence at the end of each excerpt.

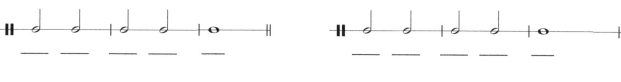

Cadence: _____   Cadence: _____

TOTAL MARKS   /78   **CONVERTED**   %

Lesson 21

Interval Recognition (13 marks)

a) Listen to the recording and add the missing notes. Identify the intervals as marked.

1. _____ 2. _____ 3. _____ 4. _____

b) Listen to the excerpt and name the harmonic interval on the last note. _____

Discrepancies (8 marks)

Listen to the recording and identify the discrepancies. Write the corrections only in the stave above. Prior to the recording commencing the beat will be played on a woodblock.

Rhythmic Dictation (34 marks)

Listen to the recording and notate the rhythm for the pitches provided. Write in the barlines. Prior to the recording commencing the beat will be played on a woodblock.

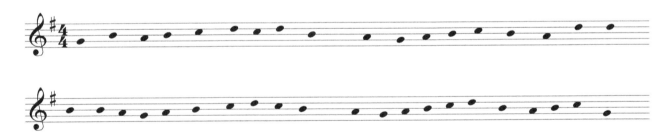

Modulation (1 mark)

Listening to the recording and identify any modulations.

No modulation _____   Relative major _____

Relative minor _____   Dominant _____

Scale Recognition (3 marks)

Listening to the recording and identify the two scales as major, harmonic minor, major pentatonic, minor pentatonic, chromatic or blues.

1. _____   2. _____

3. _____

Pitch Dictation (12 marks)

Listen to the recording and notate the pitch for the rhythm provided. Prior to the recording commencing the beat will be played on a woodblock and the tonic triad on the piano.

Melodic Dictation (18 marks)

Listen to the recording and notate the melody. Prior to the recording commencing the beat will be played on a woodblock and the tonic triad on the piano.

Chord Recognition (4 marks)

Listening to the recording and identify the four chords as major, minor, augmented or diminished.

1. _____   2. _____   3. _____   4. _____

Harmonic Progression (12 marks)

Listen to the recording and idenfity the chords used in this progression. The tonic will be played prior to the excerpt starting. Name the cadence at the end of each excerpt.

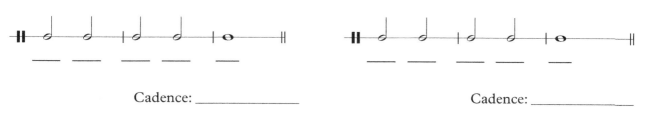

Cadence: _____   Cadence: _____

TOTAL MARKS   **/105**   **CONVERTED**   **%**

Lesson 22

Interval Recognition (13 marks)

a) Listen to the recording and add the missing notes. Identify the intervals as marked.

1. _____   2. _____   3. _____   4. _____

b) Listen to the excerpt and name the harmonic interval on the last note. _____

Discrepancies (8 marks)

Listen to the recording and identify the discrepancies. Write the corrections only in the stave above.
Prior to the recording commencing the beat will be played on a woodblock.

Rhythmic Dictation (18 marks)

Listen to the recording and notate the rhythm for the pitches provided. Write in the barlines. Prior to the recording commencing the beat will be played on a woodblock.

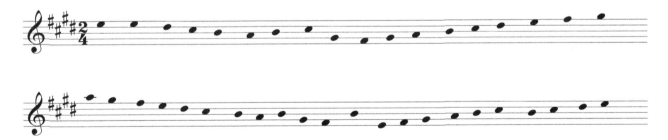

Modulation (1 mark)

Listening to the recording and identify any modulations.

No modulation _____   Relative major _____

Relative minor _____   Dominant _____

Scale Recognition (3 marks)

Listening to the recording and identify the two scales as major, harmonic minor, major pentatonic, minor pentatonic, chromatic or blues.

1. _____   2. _____

3. _____

Pitch Dictation (18 marks)

Listen to the recording and notate the pitch for the rhythm provided. Prior to the recording commencing the beat will be played on a woodblock and the tonic triad on the piano.

Melodic Dictation (18 marks)

Listen to the recording and notate the melody. Prior to the recording commencing the beat will be played on a woodblock and the tonic triad on the piano.

Chord Recognition (4 marks)

Listening to the recording and identify the four chords as major, minor, augmented or diminished.

1. _____   2. _____   3. _____   4. _____

Harmonic Progression (12 marks)

Listen to the recording and idenfity the chords used in this progression. The tonic will be played prior to the excerpt starting. Name the cadence at the end of each excerpt.

Cadence: _____   Cadence: _____

TOTAL MARKS   /95   **CONVERTED**   %

Lesson 23

Interval Recognition (13 marks)

a) Listen to the recording and add the missing notes. Identify the intervals as marked.

1. _____ 2. _____ 3. _____ 4. _____

b) Listen to the excerpt and name the harmonic interval on the last note. _____

Discrepancies (8 marks)

Listen to the recording and identify the discrepancies. Write the corrections only in the stave above.
Prior to the recording commencing the beat will be played on a woodblock.

Rhythmic Dictation (18 marks)

Listen to the recording and notate the rhythm for the pitches provided. Write in the barlines. Prior to the
recording commencing the beat will be played on a woodblock.

Modulation (1 mark)

Listening to the recording and identify any modulations.

No modulation _____   Relative major _____

Relative minor _____   Dominant _____

Scale Recognition (3 marks)
Listening to the recording and identify the two scales as major, harmonic minor, major pentatonic, minor pentatonic, chromatic or blues.

1. _____   2. _____

3. _____

Pitch Dictation (12 marks)
Listen to the recording and notate the pitch for the rhythm provided. Prior to the recording commencing the beat will be played on a woodblock and the tonic triad on the piano.

Melodic Dictation (17 marks)
Listen to the recording and notate the melody. Prior to the recording commencing the beat will be played on a woodblock and the tonic triad on the piano.

Chord Recognition (4 marks)
Listening to the recording and identify the four chords as major, minor, augmented or diminished.

1. _____   2. _____   3. _____   4. _____

Harmonic Progression (12 marks)
Listen to the recording and idenfity the chords used in this progression. The tonic will be played prior to the excerpt starting. Name the cadence at the end of each excerpt.

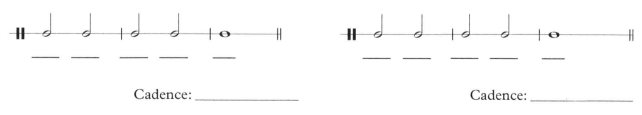

Cadence: _____   Cadence: _____

TOTAL MARKS   /88   **CONVERTED**   %

Lesson 24

Interval Recognition (13 marks)

a) Listen to the recording and add the missing notes. Identify the intervals as marked.

1. _____ 2. _____ 3. _____ 4. _____

b) Listen to the excerpt and name the harmonic interval on the last note. _____

Discrepancies (8 marks)

Listen to the recording and identify the discrepancies. Write the corrections only in the stave above.
Prior to the recording commencing the beat will be played on a woodblock.

Rhythmic Dictation (34 marks)

Listen to the recording and notate the rhythm for the pitches provided. Write in the barlines. Prior to the
recording commencing the beat will be played on a woodblock.

Modulation (1 mark)

Listening to the recording and identify any modulations.

No modulation _____   Relative major _____

Relative minor _____   Dominant _____

Scale Recognition (3 marks)

Listening to the recording and identify the two scales as major, harmonic minor, major pentatonic, minor pentatonic, chromatic or blues.

1. _____   2. _____

3. _____

Pitch Dictation (18 marks)

Listen to the recording and notate the pitch for the rhythm provided. Prior to the recording commencing the beat will be played on a woodblock and the tonic triad on the piano.

Melodic Dictation (19 marks)

Listen to the recording and notate the melody. Prior to the recording commencing the beat will be played on a woodblock and the tonic triad on the piano.

Chord Recognition (4 marks)

Listening to the recording and identify the four chords as major, minor, augmented or diminished.

1. _____   2. _____   3. _____   4. _____

Harmonic Progression (12 marks)

Listen to the recording and idenfity the chords used in this progression. The tonic will be played prior to the excerpt starting. Name the cadence at the end of each excerpt.

Cadence: _____   Cadence: _____

TOTAL MARKS   **/112**   **CONVERTED**   **%**

Lesson 25

Interval Recognition (13 marks)

a) Listen to the recording and add the missing notes. Identify the intervals as marked.

1._____   2._____   3._____   4._____

b) Listen to the excerpt and name the harmonic interval on the last note. _____

Discrepancies (8 marks)

Listen to the recording and identify the discrepancies. Write the corrections only in the stave above.
Prior to the recording commencing the beat will be played on a woodblock.

Rhythmic Dictation (18 marks)

Listen to the recording and notate the rhythm for the pitches provided. Write in the barlines. Prior to the
recording commencing the beat will be played on a woodblock.

Modulation (1 mark)

Listening to the recording and identify any modulations.

No modulation   _____   Relative major   _____

Relative minor   _____   Dominant   _____

Scale Recognition (3 marks)

Listening to the recording and identify the two scales as major, harmonic minor, major pentatonic, minor pentatonic, chromatic or blues.

1. _____   2. _____

3. _____

Pitch Dictation (15 marks)

Listen to the recording and notate the pitch for the rhythm provided. Prior to the recording commencing the beat will be played on a woodblock and the tonic triad on the piano.

Melodic Dictation (19 marks)

Listen to the recording and notate the melody. Prior to the recording commencing the beat will be played on a woodblock and the tonic triad on the piano.

Chord Recognition (4 marks)

Listening to the recording and identify the four chords as major, minor, augmented or diminished.

1. _____   2. _____   3. _____   4. _____

Harmonic Progression (12 marks)

Listen to the recording and idenfity the chords used in this progression. The tonic will be played prior to the excerpt starting. Name the cadence at the end of each excerpt.

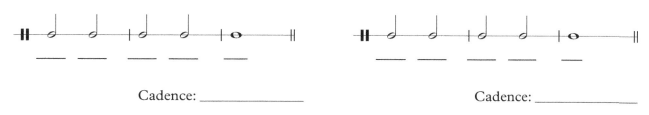

Cadence: _____   Cadence: _____

TOTAL MARKS   /93   **CONVERTED**   %

Lesson 26

Interval Recognition (13 marks)

a) Listen to the recording and add the missing notes. Identify the intervals as marked.

1. _____   2. _____   3. _____   4. _____

b) Listen to the excerpt and name the harmonic interval on the last note. _____

Discrepancies (8 marks)

Listen to the recording and identify the discrepancies. Write the corrections only in the stave above. Prior to the recording commencing the beat will be played on a woodblock.

Rhythmic Dictation (18 marks)

Listen to the recording and notate the rhythm for the pitches provided. Write in the barlines. Prior to the recording commencing the beat will be played on a woodblock.

Modulation (1 mark)

Listening to the recording and identify any modulations.

No modulation _____   Relative major _____

Relative minor _____   Dominant _____

Scale Recognition (3 marks)

Listening to the recording and identify the two scales as major, harmonic minor, major pentatonic, minor pentatonic, chromatic or blues.

1. _____   2. _____

3. _____

Pitch Dictation (16 marks)

Listen to the recording and notate the pitch for the rhythm provided. Prior to the recording commencing the beat will be played on a woodblock and the tonic triad on the piano.

Melodic Dictation (18 marks)

Listen to the recording and notate the melody. Prior to the recording commencing the beat will be played on a woodblock and the tonic triad on the piano.

Chord Recognition (4 marks)

Listening to the recording and identify the four chords as major, minor, augmented or diminished.

1. _____   2. _____   3. _____   4. _____

Harmonic Progression (12 marks)

Listen to the recording and idenfity the chords used in this progression. The tonic will be played prior to the excerpt starting. Name the cadence at the end of each excerpt.

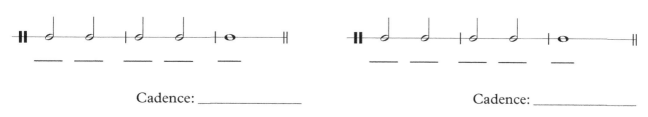

Cadence: _____   Cadence: _____

TOTAL MARKS   **/93**   **CONVERTED**   **%**

Lesson 27

Interval Recognition (13 marks)

a) Listen to the recording and add the missing notes. Identify the intervals as marked.

1. _____ 2. _____ 3. _____ 4. _____

b) Listen to the excerpt and name the harmonic interval on the last note. _____

Discrepancies (8 marks)

Listen to the recording and identify the discrepancies. Write the corrections only in the stave above.
Prior to the recording commencing the beat will be played on a woodblock.

Rhythmic Dictation (34 marks)

Listen to the recording and notate the rhythm for the pitches provided. Write in the barlines. Prior to the recording commencing the beat will be played on a woodblock. Write in the barlines.

Modulation (1 mark)

Listening to the recording and identify any modulations.

No modulation _____   Relative major _____

Relative minor _____   Dominant _____

Scale Recognition (3 marks)

Listening to the recording and identify the two scales as major, harmonic minor, major pentatonic, minor pentatonic, chromatic or blues.

1. _____   2. _____

3. _____

Pitch Dictation (13 marks)

Listen to the recording and notate the pitch for the rhythm provided. Prior to the recording commencing the beat will be played on a woodblock and the tonic triad on the piano.

Melodic Dictation (17 marks)

Listen to the recording and notate the melody. Prior to the recording commencing the beat will be played on a woodblock and the tonic triad on the piano.

Chord Recognition (4 marks)

Listening to the recording and identify the four chords as major, minor, augmented or diminished.

1. _____   2. _____   3. _____   4. _____

Harmonic Progression (12 marks)

Listen to the recording and idenfity the chords used in this progression. The tonic will be played prior to the excerpt starting. Name the cadence at the end of each excerpt.

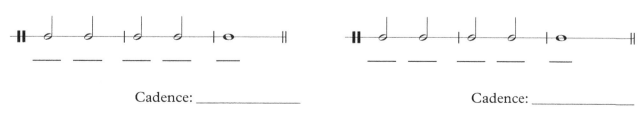

Cadence: _____   Cadence: _____

TOTAL MARKS   **/105**   **CONVERTED**   **%**

Lesson 28

Interval Recognition (13 marks)

a) Listen to the recording and add the missing notes. Identify the intervals as marked.

1. _____   2. _____   3. _____   4. _____

b) Listen to the excerpt and name the harmonic interval on the last note. _____

Discrepancies (8 marks)

Listen to the recording and identify the discrepancies. Write the corrections only in the stave above. Prior to the recording commencing the beat will be played on a woodblock.

Rhythmic Dictation (26 marks)

Listen to the recording and notate the rhythm for the pitches provided. Write in the barlines. Prior to the recording commencing the beat will be played on a woodblock.

Modulation (1 mark)

Listening to the recording and identify any modulations.

No modulation _____   Relative major _____

Relative minor _____   Dominant _____

Scale Recognition (3 marks)

Listening to the recording and identify the two scales as major, harmonic minor, major pentatonic, minor pentatonic, chromatic or blues.

1. _____   2. _____

3. _____

Pitch Dictation (10 marks)

Listen to the recording and notate the pitch for the rhythm provided. Prior to the recording commencing the beat will be played on a woodblock and the tonic triad on the piano.

Melodic Dictation (13 marks)

Listen to the recording and notate the melody. Prior to the recording commencing the beat will be played on a woodblock and the tonic triad on the piano.

Chord Recognition (4 marks)

Listening to the recording and identify the four chords as major, minor, augmented or diminished.

1. _____   2. _____   3. _____   4. _____

Harmonic Progression (12 marks)

Listen to the recording and idenfity the chords used in this progression. The tonic will be played prior to the excerpt starting. Name the cadence at the end of each excerpt.

Cadence: _____   Cadence: _____

TOTAL MARKS   **/90**   **CONVERTED**   **%**

Lesson 29

Interval Recognition (13 marks)
a) Listen to the recording and add the missing notes. Identify the intervals as marked.

1. _____ 2. _____ 3. _____ 4. _____

b) Listen to the excerpt and name the harmonic interval on the last note. _____

Discrepancies (8 marks)
Listen to the recording and identify the discrepancies. Write the corrections only in the stave above.
Prior to the recording commencing the beat will be played on a woodblock.

Rhythmic Dictation (18 marks)
Listen to the recording and notate the rhythm for the pitches provided. Write in the barlines. Prior to the
recording commencing the beat will be played on a woodblock. Write in the barlines.

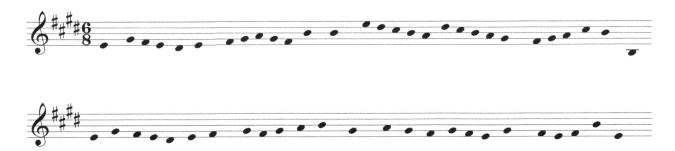

Modulation (1 mark)
Listening to the recording and identify any modulations.

No modulation _____   Relative major _____

Relative minor _____   Dominant _____

Scale Recognition (3 marks)
Listening to the recording and identify the two scales as major, harmonic minor, major pentatonic, minor pentatonic, chromatic or blues.

1. _____   2. _____

3. _____

Pitch Dictation (16 marks)
Listen to the recording and notate the pitch for the rhythm provided. Prior to the recording commencing the beat will be played on a woodblock and the tonic triad on the piano.

Melodic Dictation (20 marks)
Listen to the recording and notate the melody. Prior to the recording commencing the beat will be played on a woodblock and the tonic triad on the piano.

Chord Recognition (4 marks)
Listening to the recording and identify the four chords as major, minor, augmented or diminished.

1. _____   2. _____   3. _____   4. _____

Harmonic Progression (12 marks)
Listen to the recording and idenfity the chords used in this progression. The tonic will be played prior to the excerpt starting. Name the cadence at the end of each excerpt.

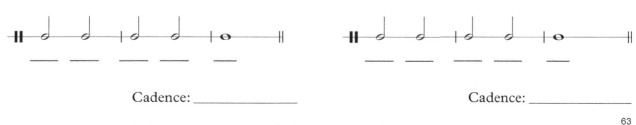

Cadence: _____   Cadence: _____

TOTAL MARKS   /95   **CONVERTED**   %

Lesson 30

Interval Recognition (13 marks)

a) Listen to the recording and add the missing notes. Identify the intervals as marked.

1. _____ 2. _____ 3. _____ 4. _____

b) Listen to the excerpt and name the harmonic interval on the last note. _____

Discrepancies (8 marks)

Listen to the recording and identify the discrepancies. Write the corrections only in the stave above. Prior to the recording commencing the beat will be played on a woodblock.

Rhythmic Dictation (34 marks)

Listen to the recording and notate the rhythm for the pitches provided. Write in the barlines. Prior to the recording commencing the beat will be played on a woodblock. Write in the bar lines.

Modulation (1 mark)

Listening to the recording and identify any modulations.

No modulation _____   Relative major _____

Relative minor _____   Dominant _____

Scale Recognition (3 marks)

Listening to the recording and identify the two scales as major, harmonic minor, major pentatonic, minor pentatonic, chromatic or blues.

1. _____   2. _____

3. _____

Pitch Dictation (16 marks)

Listen to the recording and notate the pitch for the rhythm provided. Prior to the recording commencing the beat will be played on a woodblock and the tonic triad on the piano.

Melodic Dictation (18 marks)

Listen to the recording and notate the melody. Prior to the recording commencing the beat will be played on a woodblock and the tonic triad on the piano.

Chord Recognition (4 marks)

Listening to the recording and identify the four chords as major, minor, augmented or diminished.

1. _____   2. _____   3. _____   4. _____

Harmonic Progression (12 marks)

Listen to the recording and idenfity the chords used in this progression. The tonic will be played prior to the excerpt starting. Name the cadence at the end of each excerpt.

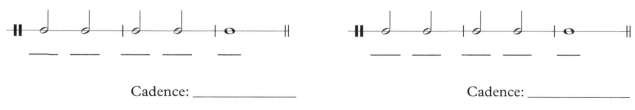

Cadence: _____   Cadence: _____

TOTAL MARKS   **/109**   **CONVERTED**   **%**

Section 2: Music Skills Development

Scale Patterns

For each of the following scales, write the pattern of tones and semitones underneath the scale.

Major/do Pentatonic

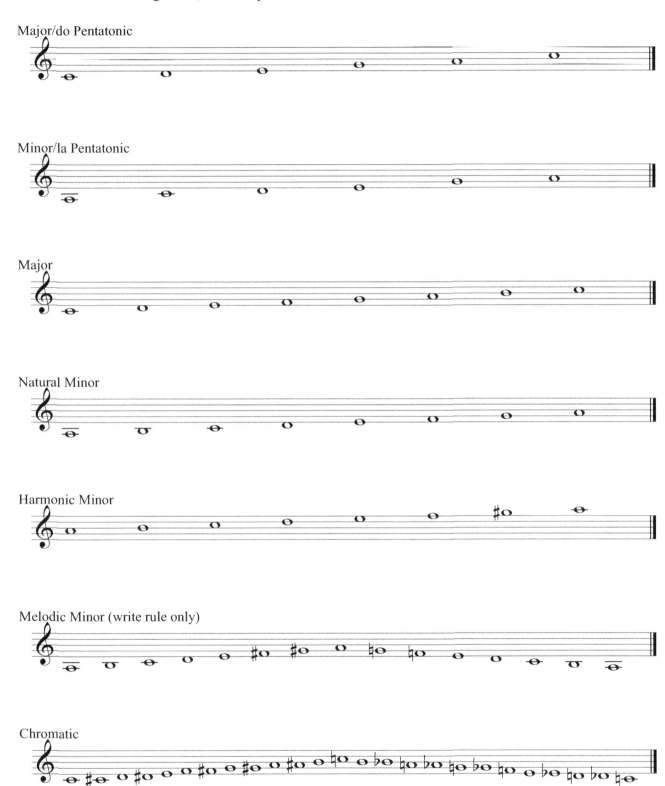

Minor/la Pentatonic

Major

Natural Minor

Harmonic Minor

Melodic Minor (write rule only)

Chromatic

Scale Degree Names

Identify the name of each scale degree in the major scale and write down a hint to help you remember them.

	Scale Degree Name	Hint
1	_____	_____
2	_____	_____
3	_____	_____
4	_____	_____
5	_____	_____
6	_____	_____
7	_____	_____
8	_____	_____

Circle of Fifths

Complete this Circle of Fifths by writing the key signatures for all major scales up to four sharps and flats. Name each key signature as shown.

C major/A minor

D♭ major/B♭ minor

C♯ major/A♯ minor

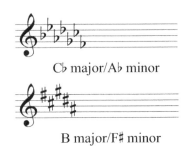

C♭ major/A♭ minor

B major/F♯ minor

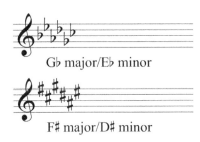

G♭ major/E♭ minor

F♯ major/D♯ minor

Scales Practice

Write the following scales in semibreves according to the instructions provided.

G harmonic minor, treble clef, ascending with a key signature

Minor pentatonic starting on B, bass clef, ascending with accidentals

Chromatic starting on E, treble clef, ascending

D melodic minor, bass clef, descending with a key signature

F major, treble clef, descending with a key signature

G major, bass clef, descending with accidentals

A flat major, treble clef, ascending with a key signature

Intervals

Hints for identifying and labelling intervals
Always label with complete name (especially with major and minor) to avoid confusion between M and m.
Always calculate the interval from the lower note.

The two types of intervals you will need to identify are diatonic and harmonic. Define these terms:

Diatonic intervals _____

Harmonic intervals _____

Diatonic Intervals

Harmonic Intervals

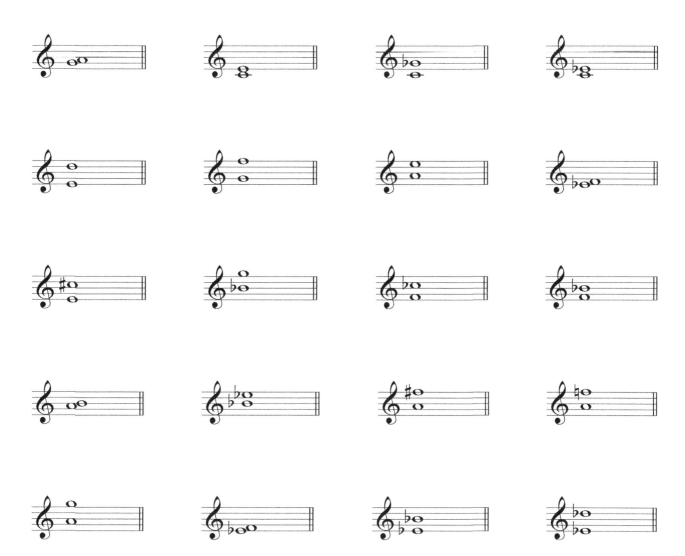

Primary and Secondary Triads

Primary triads - chords I, IV, V
Secondary triads - all other chords (ii and vi major keys only required in Year 11)

Write in the primary triads and label with Roman numerals on the scale below.

Write in the secondary triads and label with Roman numerals on the scale below.

Identify the key and write the primary triads.

Key: _____

Identify the key and write the secondary triads.

Key: _____

Identify the key and write the primary triads.

Key: _____

Identify the key and write the secondary triads.

Key: _____

Identify the key and write the primary triads.

Key: _____

Inversions

Changing the position of the tonic in the triad changes the inversion.
Root position - notes are 'stacked' in thirds
1st inversion - tonic is at the top of the chord
2nd inversion - tonic is in the middle of the chord

C major (root position, 1st inversion, 2nd inversion)

Identify the key and write the inversions for the tonic triads below.

Key: _____

Key: _____

Key: _____

Key: _____

Key: _____

Key: _____

Augmented and Dimished Triads

Major triads are made up of a major 3rd and a minor 3rd.

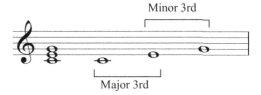

Minor triads are made up of a minor 3rd and a major 3rd.

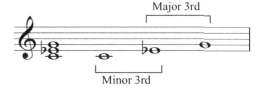

Augmented triads are made up of a _____ 3rd and a _____ 3rd.

Diminished triads are made up of a _____ 3rd and a _____ 3rd.

Identify the following triads as major, minor, augmented or diminished.

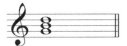   

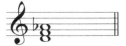   

Dominant 7th Chords

Dominant 7ths are built on what scale degree? _____

Write the dominant note for each of these key sigantures.

Using the same keys, write the dominant chord on the manuscript below.

Now write the chords, adding a 7th above the tonic. The first example is written for you.

Write the dominant 7th chord for each of these major keys. Check the clef carefully.

 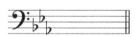  

Write the dominant 7th chord for each of these minor keys. Check the clef carefully.

Enharmonic notes

Define enharmonic _____

Write the letter name for the notes written and their enharmonic equivalent.

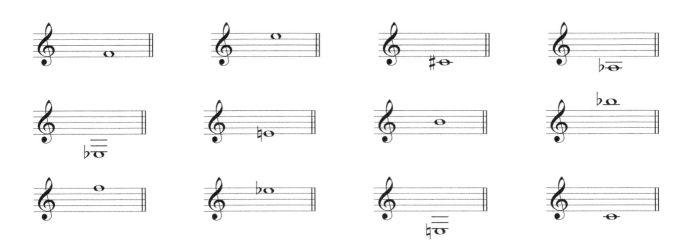

Write the enharmonic equivalent of these notes below.

78

Four-Part Vocal Style

Name the four voice types and write their range on the manuscript provided.

Four-part vocal style is also known as SATB style.

Guidelines for writing chords in four part style:
  Double the root of the chord (except for Dominant 7th)
  The bass ALWAYS has the root of the chord
  The voices shouldn't overlap (common mistake is in alto and tenor)
  Only the bass and tenor parts can be more than an octave apart

Here are six different voicings of the C major triad.

Writing chords in four-part vocal style

Note Spacing

Look at the examples below. Each one has a mistake in spacing or overlapping. Label each mistake.

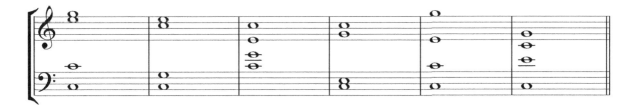

Writing Chords

Write the following chords in four-part vocal style. Remember to write the key signature.

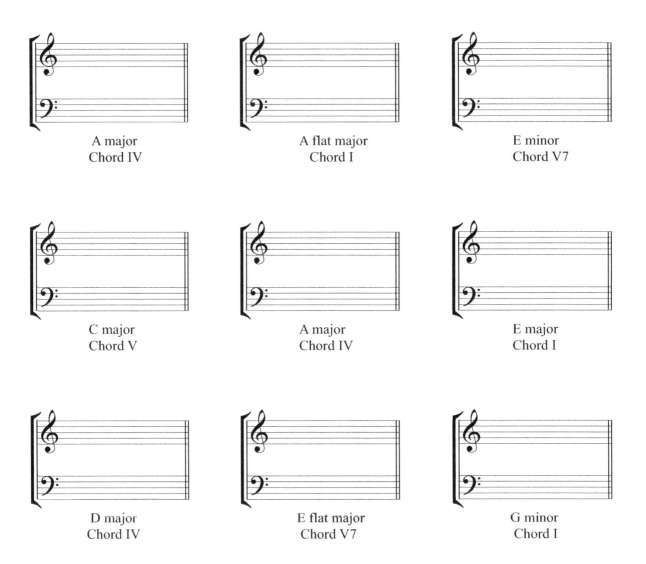

A major
Chord IV

A flat major
Chord I

E minor
Chord V7

C major
Chord V

A major
Chord IV

E major
Chord I

D major
Chord IV

E flat major
Chord V7

G minor
Chord I

Pianoforte Style

'Pianoforte style' is written with a pianist in mind, therefore the spacing of the chord needs to be practical for a pianist to play.

Three notes are written in the treble clef (i.e. a chord) with one stem for all notes (go with the majority when deciding which way the stem goes)

One note only is written in the bass, and the normal rules for stems apply.

Writing Chords

Rewrite the following chords in pianoforte style. You may need to adjust the voicing to suit.

Write the following chords in pianoforte style. Remember to write the key signature.

A major
Chord I

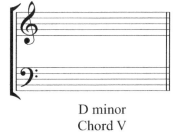

D minor
Chord V

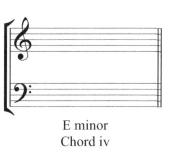

E minor
Chord iv

G major
Chord V

F major
Chord IV

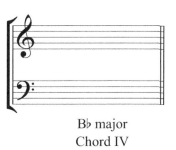

B♭ major
Chord IV

Inversions

When writing inversions of chords, the inversion is determined by the bass note. The voicing in the other parts does not matter, as long as other voice spacing rules are applied.

Inversions are labelled with numbers after the Roman numeral, as seen below.

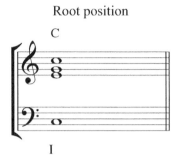

Root position

C

I

Triad in which the **root** is on the bottom. It is labelled with a Roman numeral, with no numbers after it.

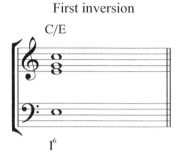

First inversion

C/E

I^6

Triad in which the **3rd** is on the bottom. It is labelled with a Roman numeral and a small '6' after it. T

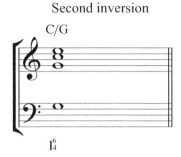

Second inversion

C/G

I^6_4

Triad in which the **5th** is on the bottom. It is labelled with a Roman numeral, and a small '6' and '4' after it.

Label these chords in C major with their chord symbols and Roman Numerals.

Write the chords indicated by the Roman numeral in the major key provided.

IV^6_4

V^6

I^6

I^6

82

Cadences - Perfect and Plagal

What is a cadence? _____

Perfect and plagal cadences are usually found where in a piece? _____

There are rules for voice leading in cadences. Follow these rules and you won't make a mistake!

Perfect Cadences (V-I)
1. Bass sings the root
2. Leading note to tonic
3. Note in common
4. Remaining voices

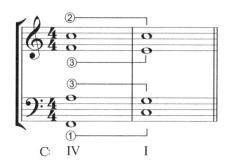

Plagal Cadences (IV-I)
1. Bass sings the root
2. Note in common
3. Remaining voices step down

Label the chords in these cadences using Roman numerals and identify as perfect or plagal.

Key: _____

Cadence: _____

Key: _____

Cadence: _____

Key: _____

Cadence: _____

Key: _____

Cadence: _____

Key: _____

Cadence: _____

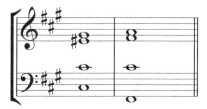

Key: _____

Cadence: _____

Cadences - Imperfect and Interrupted

Interrupted Cadences (V-vi)
1. Double the 3rd in chord vi
2. Leading note to tonic
3. 2 voices go up, 2 voices go down

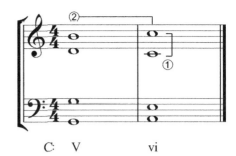

C: V   vi

Imperfect Cadences (IV-V)
1. Bass note steps up
2. Three upper parts move down

Imperfect Cadences can also be I-V

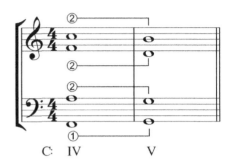

C: IV   V

Label the chords in these cadences using Roman numerals and identify the type of cadence.

Key: _____

Cadence: _____

Key: _____

Cadence: _____

Key: _____

Cadence: _____

Key: _____

Cadence: _____

Key: _____

Cadence: _____

Key: _____

Cadence: _____

Writing Cadences

For each of these major keys write a perfect, plagal, interrupted and imperfect cadence.
Label the chords with Roman numerals.

Key: _____

Key: _____

Key: _____

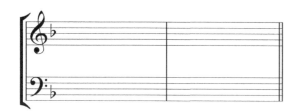 

Key: _____

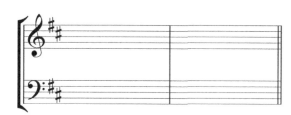 

Writing Cadences

Write perfect cadences in the following keys using pianoforte style.

Complete the following perfect cadences in SATB style (note given is the TOP note)

Complete the following imperfect cadences in pianoforte style.

Write a cadence at each of the brackets, using the bass note to determine the type.

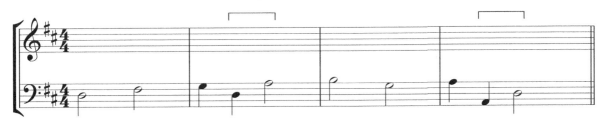

Writing Cadences over a bass line

Analysing Harmonic Progressions

To work out what chords are being used in a piece of music, you need to look at all the notes used on each beat (or bar). Once you know the notes, work out what chord is being used by stacking the notes in 3rds to make a triad.

Label the the chords with Chord Symbols above the stave and Roman Numerals below.

Recognising Modulations in Melody

The simplest way to identify a modulation is to:
- Look for accidentals
- Look for a cadence in a new key

In the melody below, the G sharp is the first non-diatonic note (note not belonging to the key of D major).

What is the relationship between D major and A major? _____

Identify the modulations in these melodies:

Tonic: _____   Modulation: _____   New Key: _____

Tonic: _____   Modulation: _____   New Key: _____

Tonic: _____   Modulation: _____   New Key: _____

Tonic: _____   Modulation: _____   New Key: _____

Types of Modulation

Common chord or Pivot chord modulation is when the chord before the first non-diatonic note can be analysed in both keys.

Modulation type: ***Common Chord***
Tonic : ***G major***
New key: ***E minor***
Relation to tonic: ***Relative minor***

Chromatic modulation is when the first non-diatonic note has the same letter name but different pitch

Modulation type: ***Chromatic***
Tonic : ***E major***
New key: ***B major***
Relation to tonic: ***Dominant***

Phrase modulation is when the change of key comes after the cadence of a section.

Exercises
Analyse this chord progression as shown above, identifying the type of modulation and the relationship of the new key to the tonic.

Modulation type: _____

Tonic : _____

New key: _____

Relation to tonic: _____

Transposition - by key or interval

There are different approaches to transposing. One of the simplest ways is to transpose by scale degree numbers.

Write out the C major and G major scales on the manuscript below, and write the scale degree numbers below each scale.

Transpose this melody in C major into G major using the scale degrees to work out the notes. Play each of the melodies when you have finished to check your work.

Transpose this melody down a perfect fifth using the same method as above.

Transposition practice

Transpose this melody into the subdominant.

Transpose this melody into the dominant.

Transpose this melody into the subdominant.

Transpose this melody into the dominant.

Transpose this melody into the subdominant.

Transpose this melody into the dominant.

Transposition practice

Transpose this melody down a minor third.

Transpose this melody up a major third.

Transpose this melody up a minor third.

Transpose this melody down a major third.

Transpose this melody down a minor sixth.

Transpose this melody up a major second.

Transposition - by instrument

Transposing by instruments uses the same technique, you just need to work out the key you are transposing to first.

B flat instruments - sounds 1 tone lower than written
E flat instruments - sounds a major 6th lower than written
F instruments - sounds a perfect 5th lower than written
A instruments - sounds a minor third lower than written

To transpose from concert pitch to written pitch, what interval do you need to transpose to for each of these instruments?

B flat instruments _____

E flat instruments _____

F instruments _____

A instruments _____

For each of the examples below, identify they key for written and concert pitch. Write the tonic for the written pitch in the space provided.

Trumpet in B flat

Concert Pitch: _____ Written: _____

Horn in F

Concert Pitch: _____ Written: _____

Alto Saxophone in E flat

Concert Pitch: _____ Written: _____

Clarinet in B flat

Concert Pitch: _____ Written: _____

Transposition practice

Transpose this melody for French Horn.

Transpose this melody for Trumpet in B flat.

Transpose this melody for Clarinet in B flat.

Transpose this melody for Alto Saxophone.

Transpose this melody into A flat major

Transpose this melody into B flat major.

Transposition practice

Transpose this melody into C major.

Transpose this melody into G major.

Transpose this melody into D major.

Transpose this melody into A major.

Transpose this melody into A flat major.

Transpose this melody into B minor.

Section 3: Music Skills Practice

Theory - skills practice 1

Write the following scales:

C major: treble clef in minims ascending

A harmonic minor: bass clef in semibreves descending using a key signature

Major pentatonic starting on C: treble clef in semibreves ascending

Identify these diatonic intervals.

Identify these harmonic intervals.

Write the primary triads in G major.

Transpose this melody into the subdominant.

Insert a time signature for this piece. What is the meter of this excerpt? _____

Label the chords in these progressions with chord symbols above the stave and Roman numerals below:

Key: _____

Key: _____

Write the following cadences in four part vocal style:

Perfect cadence in C major

Perfect cadence in A minor

Define the following terms:

presto _____

rallentando _____

sforzando _____

legato _____

Theory - skills practice 2

Write the following scales:

G major: bass clef in semibreves descending using a key signature

E harmonic minor: treble clef in semibreves ascending using a key signature

Major pentatonic starting on G: treble clef in semibreves ascending

Identify these diatonic intervals.

Identify these harmonic intervals.

Write the primary triads in D major.

Transpose this melody into the dominant.

Insert a time signature for this piece. What is the meter of this excerpt? _____

Label the chords in these progressions with chord symbols above the stave and Roman numerals below:

Key: _____

Key: _____

Write the following cadences in piano style:

Perfect cadence in G major

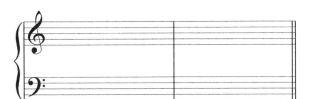

Perfect cadence in E minor

Define the following terms:

ritenuto _____

diminuendo _____

acclerando _____

a tempo _____

Theory - skills practice 3

Write the following scales:

F major: treble clef in minims ascending

D harmonic minor: treble clef in semibreves ascending using a key signature

Major pentatonic starting on G: bass clef in semibreves ascending

Identify these diatonic intervals.

Identify these harmonic intervals.

Write the primary triads in D minor.

Transpose this melody into the subdominant.

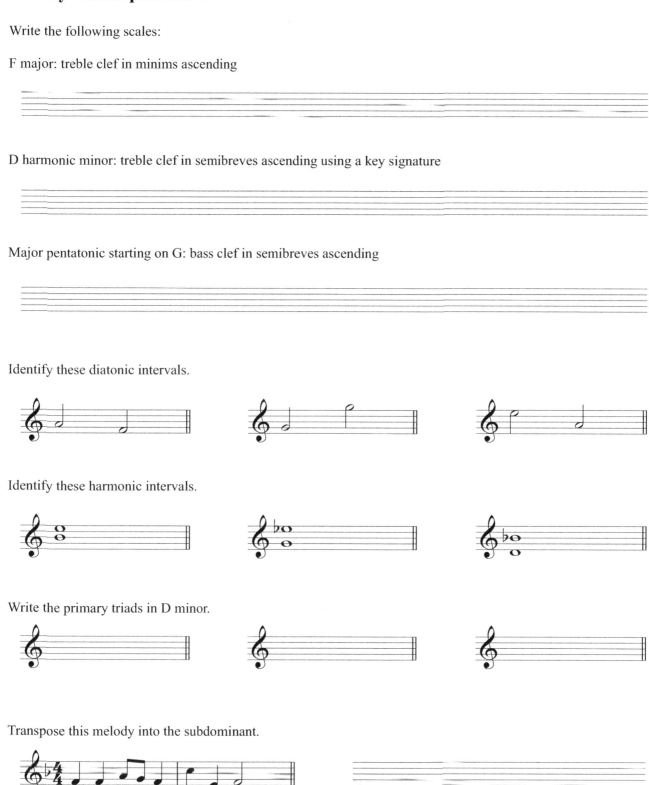

Insert a time signature for this piece. What is the meter of this excerpt? _____

Label the chords in these progressions with chord symbols above the stave and Roman numerals below:

Key: _____

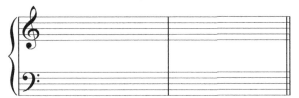

Key: _____

Write the following cadences in four part vocal style:

Perfect cadence in F major

Plagal cadence in D minor

Define the following terms:

vivace _____

allegretto _____

crescendo _____

staccato _____

Theory - skills practice 4

Write the following scales.

D major: treble clef in minims ascending

B harmonic minor: bass clef in semibreves descending using a key signature

Minor pentatonic starting on B: treble clef in semibreves ascending

Identify these diatonic intervals.

Identify these harmonic intervals.

Write the primary triads in E minor.

Transpose this melody into the subdominant.

Insert a time signature for this piece. What is the meter of this excerpt? _____

Label the chords in these progressions with chord symbols above the stave and Roman numerals below:

Key: _____

Key: _____

Write the following cadences in four part vocal style:

Plagal cadence in D major   Perfect cadence in B minor

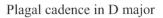

Define the following terms:

forte _____

allegro _____

pianissimo _____

lento _____

Theory - skills practice 5

Write the following scales:

B flat major: treble clef in semibreves descending using a key signature

G harmonic minor: treble clef in semibreves ascending using a key signature

Major pentatonic starting on B flat: bass clef in semibreves ascending

Identify these diatonic intervals.

Identify these harmonic intervals.

Write the primary triads in C minor.

Transpose this melody down a minor third.

Insert a time signature for this piece. What is the meter of this excerpt? _____

Label the chords in these progressions with chord symbols above the stave and Roman numerals below:

Key: _____

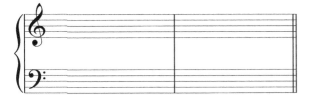

Key: _____

Write the following cadences in four-part vocal style:

Perfect cadence in B flat major

Imperfect cadence in G major

Define the following terms:

largo   _____

ritardando   _____

vivo   _____

fortissimo   _____

Theory - skills practice 6

Write the following scales:

A major: treble clef in minims ascending using a key signature

F sharp harmonic minor: bass clef in semibreves ascending using a key signature

Major pentatonic starting on C: treble clef in semibreves ascending

Identify these diatonic intervals.

Identify these harmonic intervals.

Write the primary triads in G minor.

Transpose this melody into the subdominant.

Insert a time signature for this piece. What is the meter of this excerpt? _____

Label the chords in these progressions with chord symbols above the stave and Roman numerals below:

Key: _____

Key: _____

Write the following cadences in four-part vocal style:

Interrupted cadence in A major

Plagal cadence in F sharp minor

Define the following terms:

andante _____

piano _____

adagio _____

decrescendo _____

Theory - skills practice 7

Write the following scales:

E flat major: treble clef in semibreves descending using a key signature

C harmonic minor: bass clef in semibreves descending using a key signature

Major pentatonic starting on E flat: treble clef in semibreves descending

Identify these diatonic intervals.

Identify these harmonic intervals.

Write the primary triads in E flat major.

Transpose this melody down a minor sixth.

Insert a time signature for this piece. What is the meter of this excerpt? _____

Label the chords in these progressions with chord symbols above the stave and Roman numerals below:

Key: _____

Key: _____

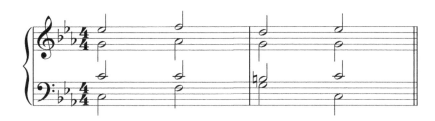

Write the following cadences in four-part vocal style:

Plagal cadence in E flat major

Imperfect cadence in C minor

Define the following terms:

mezzo piano   _____

moderato   _____

adagio   _____

crescendo   _____

Theory - skills practice 8

Write the following scales:

E major: treble clef in crotchets ascending with a key signature

C sharp harmonic minor: bass clef in semibreves ascending using a key signature

C sharp natural minor: treble clef in semibreves ascending using accidentals

Identify these diatonic intervals.

Identify these harmonic intervals.

Write the primary triads in E major.

Transpose this melody up a perfect fourth.

Insert a time signature and bar lines for this piece. What is the meter of this excerpt? _____

Label the chords in these progressions with chord symbols above the stave and Roman numerals below:

Key: _____

Key: _____

Write the following cadences in four-part vocal style:

Perfect cadence in C sharp minor

Interrupted cadence in E major

Define the following terms:

con moto _____

meno mosso _____

staccatissimo _____

marcato _____

Theory - skills practice 9

Write the following scales:

A flat major: treble clef in crotchets ascending

A harmonic minor: bass clef in semibreves descending using a key signature

Minor pentatonic starting on F: treble clef in semibreves ascending

Identify these diatonic intervals.

Identify these harmonic intervals.

Write the primary triads in F minor.

Transpose this melody for Trumpet in B flat.

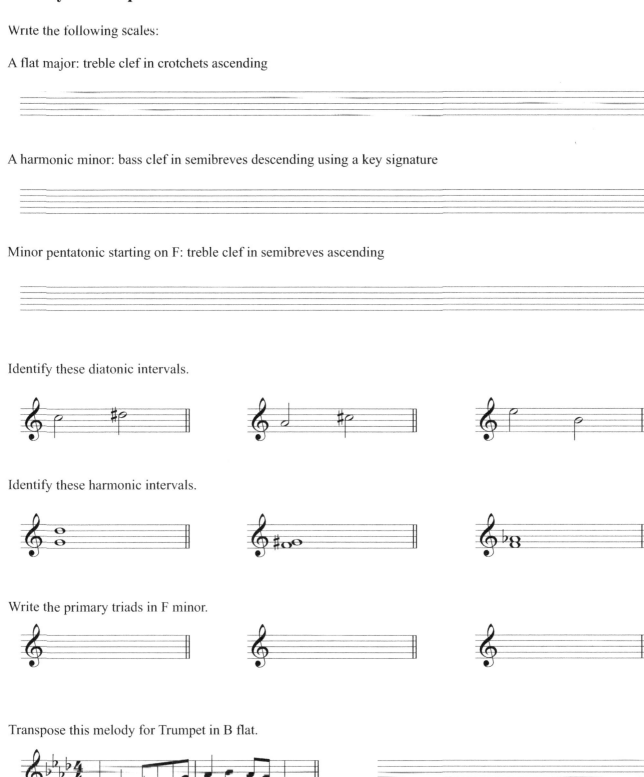

Insert a time signature and bar lines for this piece. What is the meter of this excerpt? _____

Label the chords in these progressions with chord symbols above the stave and Roman numerals below:

Key: _____

Key: _____

Write the following cadences in four-part vocal style:

Perfect cadence in F minor

Imperfect cadence in A flat major

Define the following terms:

presto _____

rallentando _____

sforzando _____

legato _____

Theory - skills practice 10

Write the following scales:

D major: bass clef in minims descending using a key signature

E harmonic minor: treble clef in semibreves descending using a key signature

F Major: treble clef in semibreves ascending using a key signature

Identify these diatonic intervals.

Identify these harmonic intervals.

Write the primary triads in B minor.

Transpose this melody for Clarinet in B flat.

Insert a time signature for this piece. What is the meter of this excerpt? _____

Label the chords in these progressions with chord symbols above the stave and Roman numerals below:

Key: _____

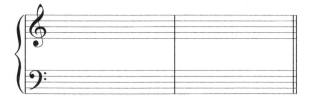

Key: _____

Write the following cadences in four-part vocal style:

Perfect cadence in F major

Interrupted cadence in E minor

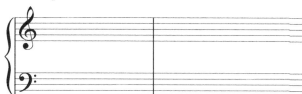

Define the following terms:

dolce _____

subito _____

senza _____

sempre _____

Theory - skills practice 11

Write the following scales:

D major: treble clef in minims ascending using accidentals

F sharp harmonic minor: bass clef in semibreves descending using accidentals

Chromatic scale starting on D: treble clef in semibreves ascending

Identify these diatonic intervals.

Identify these harmonic intervals.

Write the primary triads in C sharp minor.

Transpose this melody for Alto Saxophone.

Insert a time signature and bar lines for this piece. What is the meter of this excerpt? _____

Label the chords in these progressions with chord symbols above the stave and Roman numerals below:

Key: _____

Key: _____

Write cadences at the marked points in four part vocal style.

Define the following terms:

grazioso   _____

maestoso   _____

assai   _____

tranquillo   _____

Theory - skills practice 12

Write the following scales:

A flat major: treble clef in minims ascending using accidentals

E harmonic minor: treble clef in semibreves descending using accidentals

Chromatic scale starting on E: bass clef in semibreves ascending

Identify these diatonic intervals.

Identify these harmonic intervals.

Write the primary triads in G minor.

Transpose this melody for Trumpet in B flat

Insert a time signature and bar lines for this piece. What is the meter of this excerpt? _____

Label the chords in these progressions with chord symbols above the stave and Roman numerals below:

Key: _____

Key: _____

Write cadences at the marked points in four part vocal style.

Define the following terms:

leggiero _____

dolente _____

poco _____

largamente _____

Theory - skills practice 13

Write the following scales.

F major: treble clef in minims ascending using a key signature

D harmonic minor: bass clef in semibreves descending using a key signature

Whole tone scale starting on F: treble clef in semibreves ascending

Identify these diatonic intervals.

Identify these harmonic intervals.

Write the secondary triads in C major (excluding vii).

Transpose this melody into D major.

Insert a time signature and bar lines for this piece.

Label the chords in these progressions with chord symbols above the stave and Roman numerals below:

Key: _____

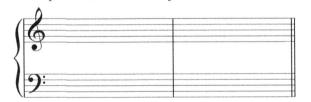

Key: _____

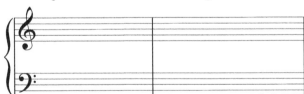

Write the following cadences in four-part vocal style:

Interrupted cadence in E major

Imperfect cadence in A flat major

Define the following terms:

andante _____

senza _____

dolente _____

assai _____

Theory - skills practice 14

Write the following scales.

A flat major: treble clef in minims ascending using accidentals

F harmonic minor: treble clef in semibreves descending using a key signature

Whole tone scale starting on A: bass clef in semibreves ascending

Identify these diatonic intervals.

Identify these harmonic intervals.

Write the secondary triads in G major (excluding vii).

Transpose this melody into A flat major.

Insert a time signature and bar lines for this piece. What is the meter of this excerpt? _____

Label the chords in these progressions with chord symbols above the stave and Roman numerals below:

Key: _____

Key: _____

Write the following cadences in four-part vocal style:

Perfect cadence in C major

Perfect cadence in A minor

Define the following terms:

vivace _____

grave _____

con forza _____

subito _____

Theory - skills practice 15

Write the following scales:

E major: treble clef in minims descending using accidentals

C sharp harmonic minor: treble clef in semibreves ascending using a key signature

Chromatic scale starting on C: treble clef in semibreves ascending

Identify these diatonic intervals.

Identify these harmonic intervals.

Write the secondary triads in F major (excluding vii).

Transpose this melody into the subdominant.

Insert a time signature and bar lines for this piece.

Label the chords in these progressions with chord symbols above the stave and Roman numerals below:

Key: _____

Key: _____

Write the following cadences in four-part vocal style:

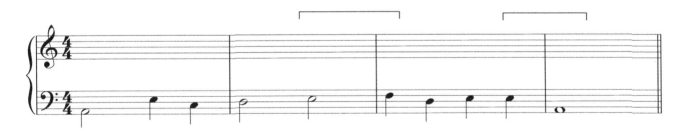

Define the following terms:

maestoso _____

marcato _____

meno mosso _____

con fuoco _____

Theory - skills practice 16

Write the following scales:

A major: bass clef in minims ascending using accidentals

B harmonic minor: bass clef in semibreves descending using a key signature

Chromatic scale starting on G: treble clef in semibreves ascending

Identify these diatonic intervals.

Identify these harmonic intervals.

Write the secondary triads in D major (excluding vii).

Transpose this melody into B minor.

Insert a time signature and bar lines for this piece. What is the meter of this excerpt? _____ _____

Label the chords in these progressions with chord symbols above the stave and Roman numerals below.
Name the modulation type (pivot chord or chromatic) and relationship between the two keys.

Modulation type: _____

Tonic: _____

New key: _____

Relationship: _____

Modulation type: _____

Tonic: _____

New key: _____

Relationship: _____

Write the following cadences in four-part vocal style:

Perfect cadence in C major

Perfect cadence in A minor

Define the following terms:

vivo _____

grazioso _____

piu mosso _____

alla marcia _____

Theory - skills practice 17

Write the following scales.

D major: bass clef in minims ascending using accidentals

E harmonic minor: treble clef in semibreves ascending using a key signature

Chromatic scale starting on F: treble clef in semibreves ascending

Identify these diatonic intervals.

Identify these harmonic intervals.

Write the secondary triads in B flat major (excluding vii).

Transpose this melody into G major.

Insert a time signature and bar lines for this piece. What is the meter of this excerpt? _____

Label the chords in these progressions with chord symbols above the stave and Roman numerals below.
Name the modulation type (pivot chord or chromatic) and relationship between the two keys.

Modulation type: _____

Tonic: _____

New key: _____

Relationship: _____

Modulation type: _____

Tonic: _____

New key: _____

Relationship: _____

Write the following cadences in four-part vocal style:

Define the following terms:

tranquillo _____

scherzando _____

marcato _____

ritardando _____

133

Theory - skills practice 18

Write the following scales:

F major: bass clef in minims ascending using accidentals

F sharp harmonic minor: treble clef in semibreves descending using a key signature

Chromatic scale starting on B: bass clef in semibreves descending

Identify these diatonic intervals.

Identify these harmonic intervals.

Write the secondary triads in A minor (excluding vii).

Transpose this melody into G minor.

Insert a time signature and bar lines for this piece. What is the meter of this excerpt? _____

Label the chords in these progressions with chord symbols above the stave and Roman numerals below.
Name the modulation type (pivot chord or chromatic) and relationship between the two keys.

Modulation type: _____

Tonic: _____

New key: _____

Relationship: _____

Modulation type: _____

Tonic: _____

New key: _____

Relationship: _____

Write the following cadences in four-part vocal style:

Define the following terms:

dolce   _____

sempre   _____

con sordino   _____

lento   _____

Theory - skills practice 19

Write the following scales:

B flat major: bass clef in minims ascending using accidentals

F harmonic minor: treble clef in semibreves ascending using a key signature

Chromatic scale starting on D: bass clef in semibreves ascending

Identify these diatonic intervals.

Identify these harmonic intervals.

Write the secondary triads in E minor (excluding vii).

Transpose this melody into B minor.

Insert a time signature for this piece. What is the meter of this excerpt? _____

Label the chords in these progressions with chord symbols above the stave and Roman numerals below.
Name the modulation type (pivot chord or chromatic) and relationship between the two keys.

Modulation type: _____

Tonic: _____

New key: _____

Relationship: _____

Modulation type: _____

Tonic: _____

New key: _____

Relationship: _____

Write cadences at the marked points in four part vocal style.

Write the Italian term for the definitions given.

Smoothly joined well connected   _____

little   _____

In a singing style   _____

mournful   _____

Theory - skills practice 20

Write the following scales:

E major: treble clef in minims ascending using accidentals

D harmonic minor: bass clef in semibreves descending using a key signature

Whole tone scale starting on F: treble clef in semibreves ascending

Identify these diatonic intervals.

Identify these harmonic intervals.

Write the secondary triads in D minor (excluding vii).

Transpose this melody into A major.

Insert a time signature and bar lines for this piece. What is the meter of this excerpt? _____

Label the chords in these progressions with chord symbols above the stave and Roman numerals below.
Name the modulation type (pivot chord or chromatic) and relationship between the two keys.

Modulation type: _____

Tonic: _____

New key: _____

Relationship: _____

Modulation type: _____

Tonic: _____

New key: _____

Relationship: _____

Write cadences at the marked points in four part vocal style.

Write the Italian term for the definitions given.

very short and detatched _____

with the mute _____

light, delicate _____

with movement _____

Section 4: Composition

Melodic Structure - Phrases

Balanced phrases were a common characteristic in the Classical period. Most eight bar phrases are made up of equal shorter phrases, forming a call and response type structure.

Look at this melody from Mozart's Minuet in F and identify the phrases.

Here is another exerpt by Mozart. Identify the sections of the phrase as antecedent (call) and consequent (answer).

Compose an answering phrase to complete this melody.

Melodic Contour

Contour refers to the shape of the melody. Commonly used contours are an arch, wave, inverted arch or pivotal (centering around a note).

Identify the contour in these extracts by drawing a line to show the contour.

Compose a four bar melody in C major that features an arch contour.

Compose a four bar melody in D minor that features an inverted arch contour.

Compose a four bar melody in G major that features a wave contour.

Continuing a Motif

When continuing a motif, it is important to keep the style consistent. One way of doing this is to repeat the rhythm or to use the same motif at the start of the second phrase.

Look at this example from Clementi's Sonatina in C and identify the elements of the original motif throughout.

Compose answering phrases to complete this melody.

Continue this motif to create an eight bar melody.

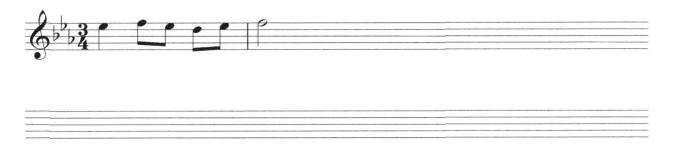

Continuing a motif - practice

Key: _____

Key: _____

Key: _____

Using a sequence

Definition: A melodic pattern repeated either higher or lower in pitch.

Example: *Twinkle, Twinkle Little Star*

Identify the sequence in this extract.

Continue this motif to create an eight bar melody that includes a sequence.

Compose an eight bar melody in D major that includes a sequence.

Melody writing for a given rhythm

Add pitch to the given rhythms, using mainly step-wise movement. Sing your melody once you are done. The key is provided for each melody. Make sure you add dynamics and phrasing to each melody where appropriate.

C major

D minor

G major

Melody writing for a given rhythm - practice

E minor

F major

D major

Writing for a chord progression

When writing melodies based on a chord progression use these guidelines:
 Use chordal notes for the strong beats of the bar
 Use non-chordal notes (passing and auxilliary) on the weak beats of the bar
 Write balanced phases
 Try to have a nice contour
 End with a perfect or plagal cadence (depending on chord progression)

In the example below, identify the chordal notes, passing notes and auxilliary notes.

Write a four bar melody using the chord progression provided using the above guidelines.

Writing for a chord progression - practice

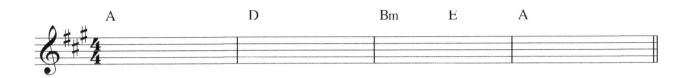

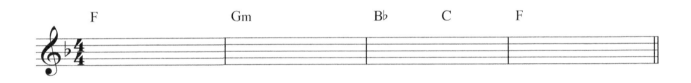

Writing a melody for lyrics

Guidelines for writing a rhythm for lyrics.

Work out where the accented syllables are - these will go on the beat
Identify a suitable meter
Write your initial rhythm - this may look quite boring!
Make your rhythm interesting by adding dotted notes

Adding your melody

Follow the usual melody writing guidelines
Remember not to use too many leaps, as your melody needs to be easy to sing
Consider using 'word painting' - reflecting the lyrics (ascending notes for going up etc)

Write a melody for the following lyrics using the guidelines above.

An autumn breeze blows through the trees,
Leaving them with no more leaves.

Writing a melody for lyrics - practice

Write a melody for the lyrics provided add appropriate tempo and dynamic markings.

Walking along the peaceful river
Watching the boats sail by

Theme and Variations

Write variations of the following melody using the variation type given.
Add tempo and dynamic markings.

Variation 1: Rhythm
Variation 2: Tonality
Variation 3: Metre

Ternary Form

This melody is the A section of a piece in Ternary form. Write a B section, and a slightly modified A section to complete the piece. Add tempo and dynamic markings.

Rondo Form

This melody is the A section of a piece in Rondo form. Write a B and C section, and a slightly modified A section to complete the piece. Add appropriately tempo and dynamic markings.

Accompaniment Styles

Vamp
A repetitive pattern, often the bass note followed by the chord as seen below.

Alberti Bass
A repetitive broken chord accompaniment with the chordal notes played in this order:
Lowest, highest, middle, highest.

Broken Chords
The notes in the chord are played in order.

Accompaniment Styles - practice

Accompaniment type: alberti bass

Accompaniment type: vamp

Accompaniment type: broken chord

Arranging for Four instruments

Guidelines for arranging:
   Ensure the parts are withing the playable range for each instrument
   Choose the correct clef
  Transpose any parts carefully
   Make sure all the beats are aligned

Arrange this Bach chorale for String Quartet.

What instrument will use a different clef? _____ Which clef? _____

Arranging for Four instruments

Guidelines for arranging:
  Ensure the parts are withing the playable range for each instrument
  Choose the correct clef
  Transpose any parts carefully
  Make sure all the beats are aligned

Arrange this Bach chorale for Wind Quartet.

Which instrument needs to be transposed? _____ Into which key? _____

Section 5: Score Analysis

1. What is the key? _____

2. What is the meter? _____

3. What scale degrees are used in the first bar? _____

4. How does the melody conclude (scale degrees)? _____

5. Add the following to the melody:

   i) A tempo marking meaning Broadly

   ii) A dynamic marking at the start of the piece indicating very soft

   iii) A dynamic marking to indicate getting louder and then softer in bars 3-4.

   iv) A tempo marking indicating to slow down over the last 4 beats.

6. Add appropriate chord symbols above and Roman numerals below the stave.

7. What is the final cadence? _____

1. What is the key? _____

2. What is the meter? _____

3. Name the intervals as marked on the score

    i)   _____

    ii)   _____

    iii)   _____

4. Add the following to the melody:

    i) A tempo marking meaning Lively and Playful.

    ii) A dynamic marking at the start of the piece indicating moderately loud.

    iii) A dynamic marking at the start of bar 3 indicating moderately soft.

5. Write the Roman numerals for appropriate chords as indicated by the asterix.

1. What is the key? _____

2. What is the meter? _____

3. Name the intervals as marked on the score

   i) _____

   ii) _____

   iii) _____

4. Add the following to the melody:

   i) A tempo marking meaning Lively and Fast.

   ii) A dynamic marking at the start of the piece indicating loud.

   iii) A dynamic marking at the start of bar 3 indicating moderately loud.

   iv) A term indicating the piece should slow down in the final bar.

   v) Appropriate phrase markings.

5. Find and label a sequence on the score.

1. What is the key?

2. What is the meter?

3. Name the intervals as marked on the score

   i) _____

   ii) _____

   iii) _____

   iv) _____

4. Add the following to the melody:

   i) A tempo marking meaning slow.

   ii) A dynamic marking at the start of the piece indicating the piece should be played softly.

5. Find and label a sequence on the score.

6. What are the final scale degrees used? _____

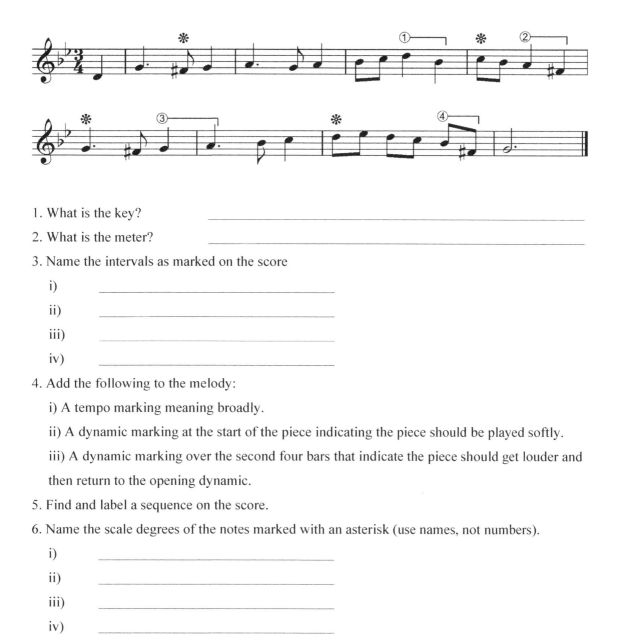

1. What is the key? _____

2. What is the meter? _____

3. Name the intervals as marked on the score

    i) _____

    ii) _____

    iii) _____

    iv) _____

4. Add the following to the melody:

    i) A tempo marking meaning broadly.

    ii) A dynamic marking at the start of the piece indicating the piece should be played softly.

    iii) A dynamic marking over the second four bars that indicate the piece should get louder and then return to the opening dynamic.

5. Find and label a sequence on the score.

6. Name the scale degrees of the notes marked with an asterisk (use names, not numbers).

    i) _____

    ii) _____

    iii) _____

    iv) _____

1. What is the key? _____

2. What is the meter? _____

3. Name the intervals as marked on the score

   i) _____

   ii) _____

   iii) _____

   iv) _____

4. Add the following to the melody:

   i) A tempo marking meaning moderately fast.

   ii) A dynamic marking at the start of the piece indicating the piece should be played loudly.

   iii) A dynamic marking at bar 4 indicating the piece should be a little softer than the beginning.

5. Name the scale degrees of the notes marked with an asterisk (use names, not numbers).

   i) _____

   ii) _____

   iii) _____

   iv) _____

1. What is the key? _____

2. What is the meter? _____

3. Add the following to the melody:

    i) A term indicating the piece should be played sweetly.

    ii) A dynamic marking at the start of the piece indicating the piece should be played softly.

    iii) Appropriate phrase markings

4. Name the scale degrees of the notes marked with an asterisk (use names, not numbers).

    i) _____

    ii) _____

    iii) _____

    iv) _____

1. What is the key? _____

2. What is the meter? _____

3. What rhythmic element is used in bar 1 and 4? _____

   What does this mean? _____

4. Name the intervals as marked on the score

   i) _____

   ii) _____

   iii) _____

5. Add the following to the melody:

   i) A tempo marking meaning very fast.

   ii) A dynamic marking at the start of the piece indicating the piece should be played loudly.

6. Name the scale degrees of the notes marked with an asterisk (use names, not numbers).

   i) _____

   ii) _____

   iii) _____

   iv) _____

1. Name the intervals as marked on the score

   i) _____

   ii) _____

   iii) _____

   iv) _____

2. Add the following to the melody:

   i) A tempo marking meaning at a walking pace.

   ii) A dynamic marking at the start of the piece indicating the piece should be played moderately loud.

   iii) A dynamic marking at the start of the second phrase that indicates the piece should be played louder than the first phrase.

   iv) Appropriate phrase markings.

3. Find and label a sequence on the score.

4. Name the scale degrees of the notes marked with an asterisk (use names, not numbers)

   i) _____

   ii) _____

   iii) _____

   iv) _____

1. Name the intervals as marked on the score

    i) _____

    ii) _____

    iii) _____

    iv) _____

2. Add the following to the melody:

    i) A tempo marking meaning lively and fast.

    ii) A dynamic marking at the start of the piece indicating the piece should be played loudly.

3. Find and label a sequence on the score.

4. Name the scale degrees of the notes marked with an asterisk (use names, not numbers)

    i) _____

    ii) _____

    iii) _____

    iv) _____

1. Name the intervals as marked on the score

   i)   _____

   ii)   _____

   iii)   _____

   iv)   _____

2. Add the following to the melody:

   i) An indication that the piece should be played majestically.

   ii) A dynamic marking at the start of the piece indicating the piece should be played loudly,

   with the second phrase moderately loud.

   iv) Appropriate phrasing.

3. Find and label a sequence on the score.

4. Name the scale degrees of the notes marked with an asterisk (use names, not numbers)

   i)   _____

   ii)   _____

   iii)   _____

   iv)   _____

1. Name the intervals as marked on the score

   i) _____

   ii) _____

   iii) _____

   iv) _____

2. Add the following to the melody:

   i) An indication that the piece be played in an animated manner.

   ii) A dynamic marking at the start of the piece indicating the piece should be played
   moderately loudly.

3. Name the scale degrees of the notes marked with an asterisk (use names, not numbers)

   i) _____

   ii) _____

   iii) _____

   iv) _____

4. Find and label a sequence on the score

1. Name the intervals as marked on the score

   i) _____

   ii) _____

   iii) _____

   iv) _____

2. Add the following to the melody:

   i) A tempo marking meaning moderately fast.

   ii) A dynamic marking at the start of the piece indicating the piece should be very loud.

3. Name the scale degrees of the notes marked with an asterisk (use names, not numbers)

   i) _____

   ii) _____

   iii) _____

   iv) _____

1. Name the intervals as marked on the score

   i) _____

   ii) _____

   iii) _____

   iv) _____

2. Add the following to the melody:

   i) A tempo marking meaning moderately.

   ii) A dynamic marking at the start of the piece indicating the piece should be very soft.

3. Name the scale degrees of the notes marked with an asterisk (use names, not numbers)

   i) _____

   ii) _____

   iii) _____

   iv) _____

1. Name the intervals as marked on the score

   i) _____

   ii) _____

   iii) _____

   iv) _____

2. Add the following to the melody:

   i) A tempo marking meaning slowly.

   ii) A dynamic marking at the start of the piece indicating the piece should be very soft.

Study the excerpt below and answer the following questions.

1. What rhythmic element is used throughout this excerpt? _____

2. What period is this piece from and why? _____

   _____ _____ _____

3. What is the accompaniment style in the opening four bars? _____

4. Describe the harmony in bars 5-8. _____

5. Define the following terms:

   Rubato _____

   legato _____

   cresc _____

6. Find an example of repetition and label it on the score.

7. Find an example of a sequence and label it on the score.

8. Name a possible composer for this work _____

1. What is the key? _____

2. Name the intervals as marked on the score.

    1) _____
    2) _____
    3) _____
    4) _____

3. What rhythmic element is used in bars 2-3? _____

4. What is the ornament in bar 2 and 4 called? What does this indicate? _____
    _____

5. What is the ornament in bar 11 called? What does this indicate? _____

6. What compositional device is used in bars 17-21? _____

7. What era is this piece from? _____

    Using the following elements of music, identify characteristics of this era in the piece,
    providing bar numbers to justify your answer.

Melody: _____

_____

_____

Rhythm: _____

_____

_____

1. Identify the intervals as marked on the score

   1) _____

   2) _____

   3) _____

   4) _____

2. Name the chords used in the following bars.

   bar 1) _____

   bar 2) _____

   bar 5) _____

3. Identify and label a sequence on the score.

4. What era is this piece from? _____

   Using the following elements of music, identify characteristics of this era in the piece, providing bar numbers to justify your answer.

Melody: _____

_____

_____

Rhythm: _____

_____

_____

1. What is the tempo? _____

2. What rhythmic element is used throughout the piece? _____

3. What is the accompaniment style? _____

4. How does the piece begin? _____

    What does this mean? _____

5. Identify the intervals as marked on the score

    1) _____

    2) _____

    3) _____

    4) _____

6. Name the chords used in the following bars.

    bar 1) _____

    bar 2) _____

    bar 5) _____

1. What is the meter? _____

2. What is the key _____

3. What accompaniment style is used throughout the piece? _____

4. What are the chords in the final bar? _____

5. Identify and define the articulation used in bars 9 and 16.

   _____

   _____

6. Identify the intervals as marked on the score.

   1) _____

   2) _____

   3) _____

   4) _____

7. Name the chords used in the following bars.

   1) _____

   2) _____

   3a) _____

   3b) _____

Nicht schnell

1. What is the meter? _____

2. What is the key? _____

3. Identify and define the dynamics used throughout the score

   _____

   _____

4. What is the compositional device used in bars 23-26? _____

5. Identify the intervals as marked on the score.

   1) _____

   2) _____

   3) _____

   4) _____

6. Identify a likely nationality of the composer and give a reason for your answer.

   _____

7. What era is this piece from? _____

   Using the following elements of music, identify characteristics of this era in the piece,
   providing bar numbers to justify your answer.

Melody: _____

_____

_____

Rhythm: _____

_____

_____

1. What is the meter? _____

2. What is the key? _____

3. What is the form? _____

   Outline the sections on the score using letter names (A, B etc).

4. Identify the intervals as marked on the score

   1) _____

   2) _____

   3) _____

   4) _____

   5) _____

   6) _____

5. What era is this piece from? _____

   Using the following elements of music, identify characteristics of this era in the piece, providing bar numbers to justify your answer.

Melody: _____

_____

_____

Rhythm: _____

_____

_____

1. What is the key? _____

2. Find and label a sequence on the score.

3. What compositional device is used in the first 8 bars? _____

4. Identify the intervals as marked on the score

   1) _____

   2) _____

   3) _____

   4) _____

   5) _____

   6) _____

5. Name the triads outlined in the following bars:

   bar 4 _____

   bar 13 _____

   bar 18 _____

6. What era is this piece from? _____

   Using the following elements of music, identify characteristics of this era in the piece, providing bar numbers to justify your answer.

Melody: _____

_____

_____

Rhythm: _____

_____

_____

Allegro

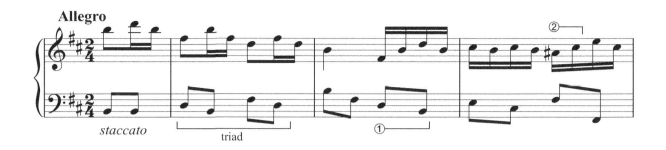

staccato   triad   ①   ②

③   ④   triad

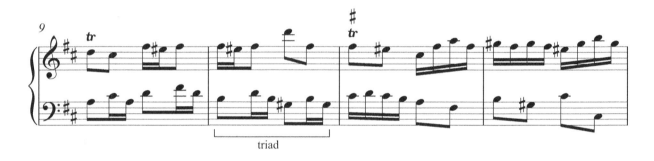

triad

⑤   ⑥

1. How is the key established? _____

2. Find and label a sequence on the score.

3. What does staccato mean? _____

4. What does allegro mean? _____

5. What does the ornament mean in bar 11? _____

6. Identify the intervals as marked on the score

   1) _____

   2) _____

   3) _____

   4) _____

   5) _____

   6) _____

7. Name the triads outlined in the following bars:

   bar 2   _____

   bar 8   _____

   bar 10   _____

1. How is the key established? _____

2. Find and label a sequence on the score.

3. What does *fz* mean? _____

4. What does *cresc.* mean?

5. What is the scale used in bar 11? _____

6. What triad is used in bar 13? _____

7. Identify the intervals as marked on the score

   1) _____

   2) _____

   3) _____

   4) _____

   5) _____

   6) _____

1. What compositional device is used throughout most of this excerpt? _____

2. Identify the intervals as marked on the score.

    1) _____

    2) _____

    3) _____

    4) _____

    5) _____

3. Find and label a sequence on the score.

4. Define the following terms:

    rubato _____

    legato _____

    cresc _____

5. What era is this piece from? _____

    Using the following elements of music, identify characteristics of this era in the piece, providing bar numbers to justify your answer.

Melody: _____

_____

_____

Rhythm: _____

_____

_____

1. What compositional device is used throughout most of this excerpt? _____

2. Find and label a sequence on the score.

3. Define the following terms:

    pesante _____

    sostenuto _____

    *piu cresc*_____

4. What era is this piece from? _____

    Using the following elements of music, identify characteristics of this era in the piece, providing bar numbers to justify your answer.

Harmony: _____

_____

_____

Dynamics and expression: _____

_____

_____

1. What is the key? _____

2. Find and label a sequence on the score.

3. Identify the intervals as marked on the score.

   1) _____

   2) _____

   3) _____

   4) _____

4. What era is this piece from? _____

   Using the following elements of music, identify characteristics of this era in the piece, providing bar numbers to justify your answer.

Melody: _____

_____

_____

Rhythm: _____

_____

_____

Section 6: Culture and Society

Compulsory Genre: _____

Research the historical development of this genre.

Composers – Compulsory Genre _____

Choose 3 composers for chosen era and outline what influenced their compositional style

Composer: _____

_____

_____

_____

_____

_____

_____

Composer: _____

_____

_____

_____

_____

_____

_____

Composer: _____

_____

_____

_____

_____

_____

_____

Using the same composers – outline their contribution to the development of the genre over at least two eras.

Composer: _____

_____

_____

_____

_____

_____

_____

Composer: _____

_____

_____

_____

_____

_____

_____

Composer: _____

_____

_____

_____

_____

_____

_____

Outline the historical development of the genre including references to the designated works and at least one other work (for Western Art Music, cover at least two eras).

_____

_____

_____

_____

_____

_____

_____

_____

_____

_____

_____

_____

_____

_____

_____

_____

_____

_____

_____

_____

_____

Identify and discuss the significance of two other works from the genre being studied.

Genre: _____

Identify and discuss the significance of another work by the composer of your designated work from the genre being studied.

_____

_____

_____

_____

_____

_____

_____

_____

_____

_____

_____

_____

_____

_____

_____

_____

_____

_____

_____

_____

_____

_____

Designated Work 1: _____

Musical Characteristics
Outline the characteristics of the period below and identify examples from your designated work.

_____

_____

_____

_____

_____

_____

_____

_____

_____

_____

_____

_____

_____

_____

_____

_____

_____

_____

_____

_____

_____

Designated Work 2: _____

Musical Characteristics

Outline the characteristics of the period below and identify examples from your designated work.

Chosen Genre: _____

Research the historical development of this genre.

_____

_____

_____

_____

_____

_____

_____

_____

_____

_____

_____

_____

_____

_____

_____

_____

_____

_____

_____

Composers – Chosen Genre _____

Choose 3 composers for chosen era and outline what influenced their compositional style

Composer: _____

_____

_____

_____

_____

_____

_____

Composer: _____

_____

_____

_____

_____

_____

_____

Composer: _____

_____

_____

_____

_____

_____

_____

Using the same composers – outline their contribution to the development of the genre over at least two eras.

Composer: _____

_____

_____

_____

_____

_____

_____

Composer: _____

_____

_____

_____

_____

_____

_____

Composer: _____

_____

_____

_____

_____

_____

_____

Outline the historical development of the genre including references to the designated works and at least one other work (for Western Art Music, cover at least two eras).

Identify and discuss the significance of two other works from the genre being studied.

Genre

_____

Identify and discuss the significance of another work by the composer of your designated work from the genre being studied.

_____

_____

_____

_____

_____

_____

_____

_____

_____

_____

_____

_____

_____

_____

_____

_____

_____

_____

_____

_____

_____

_____

Designated Work 1: _____

Musical Characteristics

Outline the characteristics of the period below and identify examples from your designated work.

_____

_____

_____

_____

_____

_____

_____

_____

_____

_____

_____

_____

_____

_____

_____

_____

_____

_____

_____

_____

Designated Work 2: _____

Musical Characteristics
Outline the characteristics of the period below and identify examples from your designated work.

_____

_____

_____

_____

_____

_____

_____

_____

_____

_____

_____

_____

_____

_____

_____

_____

_____

_____

_____

_____

_____

Section 7: Reference and Working Space

Terms and Signs

Tempo

Terminology for tempo

Adagio	Slow
Allegretto	Fairly quickly
Allegro	Lively and fast
Andante	At an easy walking pace
Largo	Broad
Lento	Slowly
Moderato	Moderately
Presto	Very fast
Vivace	In a lively way
Vivo	In a lively way
Con moto	With movement
Grave	Slow and solemn
Largamente	Broadly, fully
Prestissimo	Very quickly, as fast as possible

Terminology for modifications of tempo

A tempo	At original tempo
Accelerando	Getting faster
Rallentando	Gradually getting slower
Ritardando	Becoming slower
Ritenuto	Immediately slower or held back
Allargando	Growing broader
Meno mosso	Less movement
Più mosso	More movement

Expressive elements

Terminology for dynamics

Pianissimo (pp)	Very soft
Piano (p)	Soft
Mezzo piano (mp)	Moderately soft
Mezzo forte (mf)	Moderately loud
Forte (f)	Loud
Fortissimo (ff)	Very loud

Terminology for changes in intensity of sound

Decrescendo (decresc.)	Getting softer
Crescendo (cresc.)	Getting louder
Diminuendo (dim.)	Getting softer

Terminology for accents

Accent	stress or emphasis
Sforzando (sfz)	emphasis

Terminology for articulations

Legato	Smoothly joined well connected
Phrasing	All notes to be played legato
Slur	All notes to be played legato
Staccato	Short and detached
Marcato	Well marked
Staccatissimo	Very short and detached
Tenuto	Held on, sustained or kept down the full time

Additional terminology

Dolce	Sweetly
Molto	Very, much
Poco	Little
Sempre	Always
Senza	Without
Alla Marcia	In the style of a march
Assai	Very, extremely, in a high degree
Cantabile	In a singing style
Con forza	With force
Con fuoco	With fire
Dolce	Sweetly
Dolente	Sorrowful, mournful, pathetic
Doloroso	Sorrowfully, sadly
Grazioso	Gracefully
Leggiero	Light, swift, delicate
Maestoso	Majestically
Scherzando	Lively and playful
Subito	Suddenly
Con sordino	With the mute
Tranquillo	Tranquil and calm

Ornamentations (see additional reference sheet)

Acciaccatura	A very short grace note; crushed note
Appoggiatura	Leaning note, grace note, note of embellishment
Turn	Embellishment consisting of a group of rapid notes connecting one principal note with another
Inverted Turn	Same as a turn, but starts lower (see reference sheet)
Lower Mordent	Rapidly play the principal note, the next lower note then return to principal note
Upper Mordent	Rapidly play the principal note, the next higher note then return to principal note
Trill	A rapid alteration between the specified note and the next higher note within its duration.

Compositional devices

Ostinato	a musical phrase or melody that is repeated over and over, usually at the same pitch
Pedal	a note, usually in the bass that is sustained while other musical parts and harmonies continue
Sequence	A melodic pattern repeated either higher or lower in pitch
Imitation	the repetition of a musical idea in the part for another voice or instrument, often at another pitch and sometimes with variation
Alberti bass	a bass consisting of broken chords
Tierce de Picardie	resolving to a major key when the tonic is minor

Texture

Monophonic	One single line
Homophonic	Melody line with accompaniment, parts move together in harmony
Polyphonic	Two or more contrasting parts occurring at the same time

Signs/symbols

Barline	indicates the end of a bar/measure of music
Double barlines	often indicates the end of a section
Final barline	indicates the end of the piece
Repeat signs	indicates that the section be played again
1st and 2nd time bars	indicates how to continue after a repeat sign
Maelzel's metronome marks	indicates the tempo, the number of beats per minute
Fermata	indicates to hold the note longer that the indicated value (pause)
Coda	'End piece' a final section that adds dramatic energy to the work as a whole, usually through intensified rhythmic activity
Fine	the place on a music score that shows where the piece finishes after a repeated section
D.C. al coda	'Da capo' to be played from the beginning, and take the coda
D.C. al fine	'Da capo' to be played from the beginning until *fine*
Dal segno	To be played or sung again from the point marked with
D.S. al coda	To be played again from the sign and take the coda
D.S. al fine	To be played again from the sign until *fine*

Forms

Binary:	*Simple* – a musical form that has two complementary parts, both usually repeated *Rounded* – the B section ends with material from the A section *Extended* – additional modulations included at the start of section B
Ternary	Three part form where the first section is repeated or slightly varied in the last section, following a second, contrasting section
Strophic	Structure where all verses are sung to the same melody
Rondo	a piece of music where the principal theme is repeated between at least two sections that contrast with it, often forming the last movement of a sonata
Theme and Variations	a melody that is repeated with different variations throughout the piece of music
Minuet (Scherzo) and Trio	Dance movement where the trio is followed by the minuet, similar to ternary form
Sonata	important musical form developed in the 18th century consisting of three sections, an exposition, development and recapitulation. Used especially for the first movement of sonatas, concertos and symphonies.
Fugue	form in which a theme is first states, then repeated and varied with accompanying contrapuntal lines
Ritornello	A form where a short musical passage is used as an orchestral refrain between verses of a song or aria
Through-composed	a song with different music for each verse, especially without pauses between the verses or an opera that is not clearly divided into arias and recitatives
Cyclic	A cycle or set of movements which, though separate in themselves, form collectively one whole composition. The sonata, symphony and concerto are in cyclic form

Topic: _____   Date: _____

Topic: _____   Date: _____

Topic: _____   Date: _____

Topic: _____   Date: _____

_____

_____

_____

_____

_____

_____

_____

_____

_____

_____

_____

_____

_____

_____

_____

_____

_____

_____

_____

_____

_____

_____

Topic: _____   Date: _____

Topic: _____   Date: _____

Topic: _____   Date: _____

Topic: _____   Date: _____

Topic: _____   Date: _____

_____

_____

_____

_____

_____

_____

_____

_____

_____

_____

_____

_____

_____

_____

_____

_____

_____

_____

_____

_____

_____

_____

_____

Topic: _____   Date: _____

Topic: _____   Date: _____

Topic: _____   Date: _____

Topic: _____   Date: _____

Topic: _____   Date: _____

Topic: _____   Date: _____

Topic: _____   Date: _____

Topic: _____   Date: _____

_____

_____

_____

_____

_____

_____

_____

_____

_____

_____

_____

_____

_____

_____

_____

_____

_____

_____

_____

_____

_____

_____

Topic: _____   Date: _____

Topic: _____   Date: _____

Topic: _____   Date: _____

Topic: _____   Date: _____

_____

_____

_____

_____

_____

_____

_____

_____

_____

_____

_____

_____

_____

_____

_____

_____

_____

_____

_____

_____

_____

_____

_____

_____

Topic: _____   Date: _____

Topic: _____ Date: _____

Topic: _____   Date: _____

Topic: _____   Date: _____

Topic: _____   Date: _____

_____

_____

_____

_____

_____

_____

_____

_____

_____

_____

_____

_____

_____

_____

_____

_____

_____

_____

_____

_____

_____

_____

_____

Topic: _____   Date: _____

Topic: _____   Date: _____

Topic: _____   Date: _____

Acknowledgments

Scores Analysis

Lessons 1-15 are original melodies composed by Sarah Stopher

The following scores were used for lessons 16-30.

16. W.A. Mozart, Minuet in F, K2
17. J.S. Bach, Minuet in F No. 3 from 'A Little Notebook for Anna Magdalena Bach'
18. J.S. Bach, Two-Part Invention No. 1
19. J.S. Bach, Minuet in G No. 4 from 'A Little Notebook for Anna Magdalena Bach'
20. Chopin, Mazurka, Op. 30, No. 2
21. J.S. Bach, Polonaise in G minor, No. 10 from 'A Little Notebook for Anna Magdalena Bach'
22. Schumann, The Happy Farmer, No. 10, from Album for the Young, Op. 68
23. Schumann, First Loss, No. 16, from Album for the Young, Op. 68
24. Attwood, Sonatina no. 1 in G major
25. J. S. Bach, Badinerie from Suite No. 2 in B Minor
26. Clementi, Sonatina in G, Op. 36, No. 2
27. Handel, Water Music Suite I movement II Adagio, HWV 348
28. J.S. Bach, Prelude No. 1 in C major from 'The Well Tempered Clavier'
29. Chopin, Funeral March from Sonata Op. 35, No. 2
30. Clementi, Sonatina Op. 36, No. 1

About the Author

Sarah Stopher completed a Bachelor of Music Education at the University of Western Australia in 2004. Since then, she has worked in a country town in the North West of Australia for three years before relocating to Perth in 2008. The Aural Development Program was developed to provide her students with the opportunity to develop their aural skills at their own pace. The Stage 1 program was used with a group of Year 10 students in 2010 and proved a great success, particularly with students with little or no aural training.

Made in the USA
Middletown, DE
23 December 2020